SERIES | BOOK 1

dare to express

a collection of bold stories and brave women

CHOTSANI SACKEY   LAURA LEE LOTTO   SIMERJIT SETHI   MARY LANCASTER

JOY DANNER LEHMAN   JEN MILLER   AMANDA GOOLSBY   IVY KAMINSKY

JENNIFER WREYFORD   CHRISTY YIP   WIAAM YASIN   WHISPER JAMES

Design by Ida Fia Sveningsson

Dedication

To everyone who supported the stories in these pages—
the spouses, sisters, partners, friends, family and community members
that listened, read, and held space in its creation.

You are so appreciated and necessary for us to feel safe
enough to share hard things.

Foreword

PART 1 BY JOLIE DAWN

This was it, the moment for me to take the stage. It was a conference room with a view of the Pacific Ocean, an elevated platform which meant the whole room could see me in full view. My heart was racing and my breath was shallow. A quote was repeating in my head: "excitement and fear is one breath away." Deep breaths felt impossible to access. I was trying to steady my smile but I knew my cheeks were visibly quivering. I looked around to see a packed room of my closest friends, community members, and family. The support and encouragement felt like too much to receive. As extroverted as I am, there is just nothing that gets my nervous system jumbled and my mind racing quite like public speaking does.

After six months of full-time devotion, writing my first-ever book, this was my moment to celebrate my achievement in my own book launch party. It was time for me to stand proudly in my moment of glory, and share that I had just had a massive and unexpected success in my self-published book launch of *Empowered, Sexy, and Free*. I was twenty-five when I wrote the book and twenty-six when it was released into the world. This was by far the boldest move of self-expression and vulnerability that I had ever made in my life. It was terrifying.

My first book, *Empowered, Sexy, and Free*, was an exhibition of my most exposed stories and memories of my life. It was raw, guttural, and so very deeply personal. The book opened with the story of the moment I found out that my father had taken his life when I was just twenty years old. A bit of news that would forever change the trajectory of my life. I recounted the intensity of my childhood pain, the emotional burdens that followed me through my entire formative years, and stories of my substance abuse and addictions. The message in my book that most struck a chord with readers was the radical truth-telling, the release of victim consciousness, and the ability to find the light amongst the darkness. It wasn't just a story of pain, but the triumph in the name of it. The point wasn't just of becoming who I was meant to be in spite of trauma, but because of it. It was a deep ownership of my past as a part of my soul's journey. It showcased the resilience of the human spirit to thrive, even when life seems to serve you a big 'ol steaming pile of obstacles.

For years, I chronicled my journey with spiritual awakening and self-discovery. From meditating amongst world-renowned Indian gurus, to clocking hundreds of hours at a time in leadership development rooms, to many mad-scientist-style candlelit room sessions alone with God, discovering the secrets of the Universe. All of this wisdom, I poured into the book.

The moment when I took the stage at my own book launch party is deeply ingrained in my memory because of who I became in that moment. Jolie Dawn became a woman who was a witness to her own greatness. A woman who shared what she thought were the ugliest parts of herself and brought it to the light, in the name of other women finding inspiration and hope. A woman of fierce recognition of Self.

My book, *Empowered, Sexy, and Free*, was the start of my coaching career taking off, big time. I hit the Amazon Best Sellers list in the most competitive category, Spirituality and Self-help, ranking among the most prolific authors of our time, such as Eckhart Tolle and Marianne Williamson. The success on Amazon got me noticed by *Pacific Magazine* and I won San Diego's 'Top 30 Under 30', ranking among tech startups, visionary influencers, and multi-seven-figure earning tech moguls.

Then, on one seemingly routine workday in Austin, Texas, I got an email from a literary agent asking if I would like to publish *Empowered, Sexy, and Free* with them. I was certain the email was spam and dismissed it at first. Just three days prior was New Years Eve of 2019 and I wrote my intentions for the new year ahead. One line clearly stated: "This year I will be paid to write."

When I realized the publishing house was New World Library, and had published *The Power of Now* by Eckhart Tolle, I nearly fell out of my seat. This book was one of the most significant books on my spiritual awakening path. It was an honor beyond words to share a publisher with such a deeply meaningful book.

Writing and sharing my story has been one of the top most significant choices I've ever taken in my life. My writing career has become the backbone of my multi-six-figure per year business. It is what inspired me to launch Creatrix Publishing, my very own publishing house. I am so deeply passionate about helping other women tell their stories in the form of book writing and publishing because I know first-hand the healing that is possible.

What you are holding in your hands now is Volume 1 of the *Dare to Express* series, co-written by fourteen incredible women. Along with my co-facilitator, Alison Tugwell, I have been in a six-month writing circle, called Creatrix Expressed, and the book is our collective offering to you, our valued reader. *Dare to Express* holds twelve brave authors who similarly have met the farthest edge of their comfort zone in the name of telling their stories. Bold. Honest. Uncut. They have dared to express.

Storytelling is an ancient art of wisdom-sharing that dates back to the beginning of humanity. Storytelling stays with us, etched in our memories, and it transcends time. This is our intention in sharing with you, that you may have an experience through these words that gives you just the medicine that you seek at this time in your life.

Dare to Express is a collection of bold and vulnerable stories by brave women who have dared to share a personal and pivotal part of their lives with you. It is our shared intention that these words land as resonant moments of wisdom and refreshing bits of truth, from our hearts to yours. We believe that if you desire to live a life of personal power and freedom, you must first have the courage to shed light on your darkest life moments.

From heartbreak to mental and physical health recovery to challenging family dynamics, and everything in between, each author has bared her soul so that you may find your own healing journey. We invite you to awaken your innate joy and spiritual clarity to discover the brightest version of yourself, and to live your life with a focus on purpose.

Diving into this book will feel like you've traveled into a cozy living room full of girlfriends recounting their wildest life experiences, divulging their most astounding plot twists, and swapping lessons from all of the professed chaos. So grab a cup of tea, light some candles and palo santo, and join us for a rich and captivating storytelling experience.

Dare to Express is for you if you desire to experience:

- *Self-expression:*
  recognize your own uniqueness and have the courage to walk your own path, unapologetically

- *Self-responsibility:*
  learn the power of your emotional intelligence to reclaim your inner peace, power, and motivation

- *Self-awareness:*
  discover your purest form of creativity, choose boldly to live in action over fear, and ditch those beliefs that stunt your growth

Dare to be the greatness that you came to Earth to be.
Dare to be the Creatrix of your own story.
Dare to share the wisdom of your life experience.
Dare to be seen in your raw truth.
Dare to Express.

Jolie Dawn

Intuitive Business Coach, 6X Amazon Best Selling Author, and Founder of Creatrix Publishing and Prosperity Queendom Inc.

Foreword

Imagine we are in another time and place; a space where *no women are strangers.*

When our paths cross, it's as if we are reuniting, instead of meeting for the first time. This world existed for me within *Creatrix Expressed.* What you hold in your hand—the words echoing in your ear—is a product of passion and persistence.

Creatrix Expressed is a six-month program in which women of all backgrounds write towards their most pivotal and healing journeys. Founded by 6X Amazon Best Selling Author and intuitive coach, Jolie Dawn, the program became an exercise in intimacy.

As the facilitator of our weekly writing circles, I was moved by the way this program strengthened my connection to, my respect for, and ultimately my deep commitment to serving women in empowering themselves through self-expression.

One of the ways I self-express is through poetry. Some might say that a photo is worth one-thousand words, but I feel like a poem is worth one-thousand images. My aim in this introduction is to create a composite of what my experience was in working with each of these women. I have grown to love every single one and admire their vulnerability, growth of character, and command of their voice through authorship.

So allow me to introduce them sequentially
as you'll meet them, via a form of Japanese poetry
5/7/5 syllables), aka, "Hi-ku."

Ivy

Rockstar Oracle
Her teenage testimony
Both frees & protects.

We begin our collective story with Ivy. In part because of the clarity of her motif.

When Ivy puts her mind to something, she shows up.

Despite child pick up schedules and shifting clients around, I do not think Ivy missed a single session of our course. She is every teacher's dream student—hungry, humble, wide-eyed, and organized. And she's got one hell of a story to share about how she came to be.

She is a living testament to the confidence that can manifest from courageous choices we make before we are ready to make them.

Sim

*Mother expecting
what she desires … ; what if
different were better?*

As an infant girl grew inside Sim for the duration of our course experience, Sim grew in her ability to articulate intimate details. I encourage you, dear reader, to let go of whatever is happening in your external environment and go with this masterful coach and writer into the hospital room with her—one of the scenes in which her story takes place. I have a feeling you will connect with every inch of this literary journey, no matter where you are in yours.

Jennifer W.

*Love warrior lessons
Wielded with wit & wisdom,
dressed up in drama!*

Everyone has a "Yes, that really happened" story. Jennifer tells hers here. It is for every woman who fears that her "happily ever after" tale will never be told. As a human, she has the same effect that her writing has— instant likeability. And although I prefer to have brunch with her in person, I got to read her words for this book in a chic, Chicago cafe over coffee and carbs; I think you will agree that any written piece from Jennifer is a worthy companion.

Amanda

*Rewriting success
for herself despite achieving
all against the odds.*

To let you in on a little inside joke about this poem, Amanda had rewritten her whole story from the first to the second draft during our time together. But it is so fitting that this athlete and business owner who had formerly "checked all the boxes" as to what is desired and expected of her would create a whole new 'checklist'. I love how bold and fearless she is and I'm excited for us both to witness her on an extraordinary path.

Laura Lee

*Fiery healer calls
"BS" and burns barriers—
Truth & Love remain.*

In our first session, Laura Lee blew me away with her passion and openness. This is a woman committed to her creation. And why wouldn't she be? A mother of four on a farm, she has a lot to be proud of in what she has cultivated. I hope her infectious energy lights a spark for your creative, healing journey, too!

Mary

Transition sister,
a vessel between worlds; yet
roots in Texas soil.

Mary's healing magic was foretold to me by Jolie, creator of *Creatrix Expressed*, who showed up on her doorstep desiring every service Mary had to offer. Meeting her in person in her hometown of Wimberley, Texas, I felt both her "otherworldliness" and grounded, nurturing presence. She and her story will capture your attention, and hold you in spaciousness and grace. Enjoy.

ChiChi

Fierce & sensitive,
a confident confidante
shares self-love secrets.

It is not hard to see ChiChi's beauty from the outside, and yet the gorgeousness of her soul shines especially bright when she shows us the cracks it comes through—her quiet vulnerability. For every woman who has not wanted to claim her body as it were, ChiChi shows us what can happen when acceptance is the aspiration.

Chotsani

*Goddess manifests
motherhood, redefines it
while listening in.*

Chotsani is who I would define as a modern-day Marvel hero. While not able to join any of our sessions live due to a demanding work schedule and tending to her son, she diligently persisted in the program. Catching replays, and sharing insights and wisdom with our fellow Creatrix sisters, she is a woman that makes it work, no matter what, and her story reflects this.

Wiaam

*Angel in hijab
unfurls her wings to fly. See?
Read All About It!*

"This song is how I feel about finally sharing my story," Wiaam shared with me about Emeli Sandé's track, "Read All About It." Like so many of us, Wiaam finds the strength to express in the lyrics of songs. I found her connection to Tupac's "Keep Ya Head Up" especially compelling as it relates to her story of survival as you will read in the pages ahead.

Jen M.

She said to the mirror:
"Mermaid-painted Phoenix, rise!"
Aho! It was so.

No one's artistic voice developed more rapidly than Jen's throughout our program experience. Perhaps it was her being in the matrimonial mindset; she was wed during this book's production in an ocean-inspired dress that not one of us could forget. Whatever it was, she seemed to take her own internal learnings and the external editorial suggestions by our team and execute wildly upleveled literary delights.

Joy

The woman we want
at our bedside and brunch,
heart & arms open

When Joy joined us, I remember getting curious about what she was doing here, provided that she was already a part of another writing group. But how generous were her shares, how big her vulnerability throughout our time together! Joy inspired me as someone steeped in service in the diverse communities within and around her Minneasota town. She gave us an example of how to show up and "leave it all on the page" as they say.

Whisper

*Even if spoken
silently, her story screams:
"Redemption's Here."*

Whisper is truly a living miracle. The first time I heard her story, I was in a program alongside her led by Jolie. There was not a dry eye in the Zoom room that day. We close our collective book with her story as a reminder to us all that your freedom, what you have overcome to live and tell on the other side, is only the beginning.

Although I don't yet know you as intimately, I know enough to know that if you were attracted to this book, *you have a story to share*, too.

Jolie and I want to know you. Please, share with us how these stories have touched, uplifted, and inspired you, especially if they have led you to take action towards a truer version of yourself.

You can do that by tagging @joliedawnxo and using the hashtag #CreatrixExpressed2022.

In the meantime, enjoy the stories from our dear friends in the *Creatrix Expressed* circle. We look forward to hearing and seeing your stories as well.

Alison P. Tugwell

Head Coach and Program Manager
of Creatrix Expressed

Table of

Contents

CHAPTER 1

Locked Up and Liberated:

LESSONS I LEARNED BY USING MY VOICE

By Ivy Kaminsky

Using my voice is not something I am known for, nor is taking up space. And, I am determined to change that. There is nothing more powerful than a woman standing fully in her power, and using her voice to speak her truth and stand up to the injustices of the world. It takes such bravery, going against so much we are taught and conditioned to do and to be as women, historically and even in our modern world.

As a child growing up, I loved to color, to crochet, to weave potholders on a loom, to make latch hook designs (remember those ugly

"I write for those women who do not speak, for those who do not have a voice because they were so terrified, because we are taught to respect fear more than ourselves. We've been taught that silence would save us, but it won't."

– AUDRE LORDE

rug looking things, circa 1979!?), to do paint-by-number art, to bake brownies in my Easy Bake Oven, to make Shrinky Dinks (designs you would color with colored pencils and then put in the oven to shrink up to small plastic ornaments). I would spend hours getting lost in my own little creative world, sewing up this or dreaming up that. My imagination was filled with bright colors and bold patterns just bursting to be expressed. And because I was an only child, I was very attached to my meager belongings, especially my art supplies.

One time, around the age of seven, my mother and I were visiting my uncle in Florida. About a week into our vacation, he came home to our stuff everywhere; my coloring books and crayons left all over the table, both of our clothes, bathing suits, and my mom's pantyhose hanging on every surface and in piles on the floor. We returned from the beach that afternoon and found him upset because we had made such a mess of his place. He said to me, "Ivy, you forgot to put your crayons and coloring books away. They were all over the table. I figured you didn't care about them, so I threw them away." My distraught seven-year-old self went right up to him, a former Vietnam soldier, and kicked him in the shins as hard as I could, not realizing he was joking and had just hidden them from me temporarily. He still tells the story of how much it hurt and how he would not do that again.

I also loved to dance and took lessons from Dee Dee's Dance Studio near my house for many years. Every year, we would have a new song and choreography to learn and to perform in front of loved ones. My favorite part, besides the dancing, was the fun costumes we got to wear. Oddly, I don't remember being terribly uncomfortable in these performances. I do remember stepping on stage with my fellow performers, excited to wear my pretty sparkling costumes, or my tap shoes, and to show off my dancing prowess. Maybe it was because it's too long ago to remember adequately, or more likely because I hadn't been fully conditioned to be afraid yet, and I could blend in with the crowd. Somehow, I figured out that performing 'in character' with the protection of the group around me was likely easier than showing up fully as myself, all by the ripe old age of nine years old.

This love of dance followed me into school as well. In seventh grade, along with studying French, I joined the French Club and became one of the French CanCan dancers; my long skinny legs were made for high kicks. I also joined a group of traditional Mexican dancers to perform around our predominantly Latino community. The best part of that was stomping around and twirling my white, flowy, full skirt to the music. I was one of two tall, painfully-skinny white girls in that group. What a strange site we must have been interspersed with all the other beautiful Latina girls.

I vividly remember my first pair of rollerskates. I got them from my mom as a gift for my ninth birthday. They were white with two royal blue diagonal stripes down the outside edge of the boots, with matching royal blue wheels and toe stoppers. They came in a thin, metal carrying case with the same blue stripes on the outside, and the forceful click that the latches would make as they locked in to secure my new prized possession was almost as exciting to me as hearing the ice cream truck on a hot summer's day.

I loved to roller skate from about ages nine to fourteen. Every weekend that I could talk my mom into allowing me to go, I would either go for a couple of hours to skate, or if I was really lucky as I got older, I could go to the overnight skate with a friend on a weekend night. On these nights, the highlight was the 'snowball,' where they would dim the lights, play a slow, romantic song, and anyone hoping to be chosen would line up along the side of the rink. I would stand there trying to be nonchalant about how badly I wanted to be chosen. I don't remember ever actually being chosen, but I was ever the hopeful optimist.

School was always easy for me. It was the one thing I knew I could do well without much effort. In the classroom, I was most comfortable sitting in the second or third row back, in the middle of the room. That way I could focus on whatever the teacher was teaching, I wouldn't get distracted by too many other students around me, and most importantly, I could try to blend in, which felt safe for me at this tender age.

Surprisingly, I was comfortable raising my hand to read out loud, likely because I loved to read. One of my favorite things to do would be to come home from the library with an armload full of books, as many as I could carry. These books allowed my imagination to roam freely and the stories allowed me to escape my not-always-wonderful reality. I think the other reason I was comfortable raising my hand in class to read was because I read so much, my vocabulary was pretty vast, and I always excelled in spelling, English, and grammar. I raised my hand at other times as well, even if it made me uncomfortable, because I always did my homework and could usually answer the teacher's questions knowledgeably.

So, yes, I was booksmart, but I think it was my emotional intelligence that really got me far. I was often the only child amongst many adults, so the conversations I did have were deeper than most. I could also sense what people wanted from me. I could morph myself into whatever they wanted, and give it to them, if I chose.

I grew up quickly, both literally and figuratively. I had such a growth spurt that I would lie in bed at night crying out in pain because my legs were growing so fast. In my second grade class picture, I was in the middle of the back row because I towered over most of my classmates by a head, even the boys. Thankfully, they would soon catch up and pass me, but at this time, I was awkwardly tall. I also had poor eyesight and had to wear glasses from first grade on. So, here I was, shy, quiet, booksmart, and awkwardly tall. (Lucky me.)

My life circumstances allowed me to grow up much too quickly, as well. As the only child of a single mother, who happened to be a functioning alcoholic that worked as a bartender to support us, I had a lot of responsibilities piled on me at a young age. My chore list was extensive. Sometimes, I joke and say she was the child and I was the adult (sad, but also true in some ways).

My summers home from school around this time were filled with late nights reading in my single bed by flashlight, so as not to alert my mom that I was still awake reading long after my bedtime. And days spent creating, doing odd art projects, or playing tennis at the courts at the park a block and a half away from home, either with a neighborhood friend or by myself, hitting the ball repeatedly against the backboard. Many times I would have to wander into the woods behind the courts to retrieve my overachieving tennis balls. The same place I would later hide as I learned to smoke Marlboro Lights cigarettes out of the view of prying eyes.

By the time my friends started to reach puberty, I was lagging behind. Or at least that is what it felt like as I waited to develop breasts that never came. I also felt like some of my girlfriends were warpspeed ahead of me where boys were concerned. I definitely wanted boys to like me, but it just didn't happen. I felt completely invisible to them. I would hear stories of others making out with boys, and I hadn't even had the opportunity to talk to one in a flirty, I-like-you-and-you-like-me sort of way.

I was thirteen years old by the time I finally felt seen by someone of the opposite sex and that someone showed interest in me at all. That doesn't sound very old to me now, but it felt ancient at the time. However, these initial adolescent fumblings were cut short by what would turn out to be one of the most pivotal experiences of my life.

● ● ●

In spite of the many days and weeks in both the social worker and prosecutor's offices preparing for the trial, my inexperienced thirteen-year-old body was in complete shock. No amount of preparation could have made me ready for this day. My memory, trying to protect that fragile young girl, holds very few solid images from that stuffy old courtroom, but the feelings I experienced in my time there have been captured like items in a time capsule and seared into my bodily cells for life.

The silence was deafening as he entered the courtroom, his hands behind his back in handcuffs. I could not bring myself to look at his ominous, threatening, pockmarked face.

When I heard my name, it took me a moment to realize I was being called to the stand. It felt like I was under a microscope being scrutinized like a fresh sample, and I think I might have stopped breathing for a moment. I finally took a deep breath and stood up from my well-oiled hardwood bench seat. To have every single person's eyes on me, as I walked the short distance to the stand, made everything seem like it was in slow motion and I was walking through heavy fog to get there. Once I stepped into the small enclosed space, stepped up to the seat, and finally sat down, I had to put my right hand up and say the oath so that my testimony could begin. The 'easy' part of the questioning came first. The State's Attorney, a very professional and kind man, who I had gotten to know a bit prior to the trial, was to question me first. He covered all of the parts that we had talked about in his office. I answered each of his questions as clearly and loudly as I could, like he had instructed me to. He still had to ask me to speak up louder a couple of times.

When he was finished with his line of questioning, he stepped down and the public defender stepped up towards the stand, the small wooden box that I was enclosed in. This is the part that no matter how much they warned me, no one could really have prepared me for. This woman of the court tried to twist my words every which way, to have the jurors and the courtroom doubt my firsthand account of that day. She basically tried to make the audience believe that I was a whore, and that I was already sexually active, and that I wanted to have sex that day with a man almost three times my age. I had to say many times and in many different ways, "No. No, that is absolutely not what happened." Oddly enough, during this part, I did not have to be prompted to speak up.

After four days it was finally time to hear the verdict (I could not wait to get this over with and get out of the spotlight). I had no idea what to expect, but I somehow knew whatever the jury's decision was, it was a big deal, and it would change my life forever.

So, on the morning of April 25th, 1985, as a full courthouse of people waited for the judgment, the judge stated that the defendant was charged guilty of rape of a minor and charged with 1st and 3rd degree criminal sexual conduct, or sexual penetration with a victim under thirteen years old. He was sentenced to 144 months in prison, which equates to twelve years. (Only now, in this moment am I realizing the significance of his sentence of one year of prison for each of my tender years of life leading up to my rape). And the hardest part of all of this for me to reconcile in my mind and especially in my heart, was that the defendant was not a stranger to me. He was a man who had taught me how to throw a football. He was a man who was supposed to care for and protect me. He was my stepfather.

As I sat in a courtroom full of people, terrified but calm, and listened to the judge deliver the verdict of 'Guilty', my immature self likely had no idea how my life and the trajectory of my life would be forever changed from that moment forward. I could not possibly realize the full magnitude of what had just happened. And there was no way to know what type of changes were yet to come.

One year later on a fateful day in the spring of 1986, the phone rang at our home. My mother answered, and I could tell instantly that it was him. It was a bad day for her, she had been drinking. He kept her on the phone for a longtime and convinced her that I had been lying about the rape all along. They began to talk regularly, him calling her from prison. After that, my mom would say things to me like, "It's ok, Ivy, you can tell me the truth."

Needless to say, all any of this did to my already angsty, budding teenage self was to hurt me, confuse me, make me want to be anywhere but home, and to make poor choices. I was already smoking cigarettes, and experimenting with alcohol and marijuana, and now I started to ditch school and run away, usually on the weekends when I didn't want to come home. One time while I was babysitting for one of my mom's girlfriend's children, she was talking to her friend after they came home from the bar. I overheard her saying about me: "she'll probably be pregnant by the time she's sixteen."

(Later, my mother didn't remember saying this, but it was one of the most hurtful things I've ever heard said about me, especially by someone who was supposed to love and protect me.) However, as much as this, the rape, and the trial hurt me, together they were also a huge wake-up call. It didn't sink in right away though. I would continue to be in and out of shelter homes and experimenting with drugs and alcohol until I finally landed in a good permanent foster home, where I basically stayed until I graduated from community college. I had to find my own way, but somewhere deep down I was determined to prove my mother and anyone else who didn't believe in me wrong, and more importantly, to prove myself right.

● ● ●

My life after that significant time in my personal history has been simultaneously beautiful, extraordinary, and tragic. I have had to learn the hard way, with the death of my mother, my father, all of my grandparents, and a child at full-term, that life is way too short, not to be lived fully. So, as a grown woman, I tend to go big when I do scary things; no small baby steps for me, just a huge step off a sheer cliff into the abyss. The first time I attempted to get over my fear of public speaking was at a pitch competition for a large well-known start-up accelerator that happened annually at a university. I stood up in front of an auditorium full of my social entrepreneurial peers and tried to articulate my new nonprofit business plan, professionally and concisely. As I stood there, my anxiety grew until my voice was audibly shaky and I kept forgetting to breathe. I fumbled through the first part, but by the time it came to Q&A, I could barely keep my voice steady enough to speak. And the feeling of all eyes on me, knowing I completely bombed, made me feel small and weak, and I so desperately wanted to go find a hole to crawl into to nurse my wounds, like a feral cat. When I was finally able to escape, I walked away as quickly as I could without running, trying to keep my tears at bay. I was wondering what in the hell possessed me to speak in front of such a large group like that when a young guy caught up to me to ask a couple of questions, introduce himself, and offer me his business card. I am sure that he felt sorry for me, and I couldn't wait to get out of his sight, so I could go cry, sit in my shame, and process what had just happened. I never was able to listen to the recording of that 'speech' and I never attended that event again; it was just too painful to face.

Another time I thought I would try a different approach to face my fear. Even though I'm terrified of public speaking, some part of me thoroughly enjoys singing. I love singing in the shower, in the car, and even in the front of my cardio step class at the gym (but only loud enough so the people in my immediate vicinity can hear). So, I thought why not use that love of singing to help tackle the fear of being onstage? And maybe it's just me, but doesn't everyone have a secret dream of being a rockstar?

It had taken me until I was forty-seven years old, but I had quit drinking for a year. My decision was based on the fact that even if I had one drink I would feel depressed the next day. And one night after having way too many drinks at a holiday party, and doing some really stupid things involving a guy that was so not worth my time, including making out with him in the bathroom when he had come with another woman and driving drunk when I was supposed to be sleeping at a friends to avoid that, I decided enough was enough. Time for some big changes! I was tired of 'giving myself away' to crappy men, feeling lonely, depressed, and not doing the things I really wanted to do. So, in my usual bold, jump-off-the-cliff form, I decided to quit drinking for at least one year (to make sure I actually could, because to be honest, I wasn't really sure). This big decision gave me free reign to say yes to every scary thing that came my way, or that I had always wanted to do. I remember thinking, this is my year. There will be no holding back. I will do this thing wholeheartedly as a life experiment and see if it makes a difference in my life.

A couple of months later, as I was sitting at my computer, clicking away on the keyboard, an email message popped up in front of me. It stopped me frozen. My heart started to pound wildly with excitement. I had to read it more than once. So many emotions flooded through my body simultaneously; exhilaration, surprise, fear, wonder, and anticipation. It was only one week before the Women's Rock n Roll Retreat and, holy shit, I was 'in'! At that moment I knew that I was about to embark on a wild ride that would forever change me (and it was time to 'buckle up buttercup').

As I sat in the packed room, looking around and listening to the eclectic collection of creatives, moms, teachers, and musicians, my heart doing occasional somersaults in my chest, I was nervous about what lay ahead. I didn't regret my decision, I was just terrified of the unknown and thinking to myself, "How the hell are they going to turn us group of misfit wannabes into a rock band??"

At the end of the first long, grueling day, I think all of us wanted to quit. We were facing extreme pressure. We had to learn our instrument (voice in my case), write two original songs, and learn to play them, plus a cover song. Then, we were to perform our new songs in front of a live audience, in just two short days. All of this, as complete novices and strangers, felt like more than any of us could bear.

Add to that, the fact that I couldn't sleep much because of the anxiety of knowing I would have to be performing onstage very soon. But, I kept showing up and so did everyone else. There were voice lessons with my badass vocal coach, group practices, and some really fun song writing sessions. We got together in small groups and were shown how fun and easy song writing could be. We would pick a theme, a general genre or mood we were going for, all write down some potential lines of song lyrics, pick our favorites, and string them together with a good beat, a melody, or a chorus. The most surprising part for me was that I turned out to be a natural at writing song lyrics and I actually loved doing it.

And somehow we pulled it all together.

On the final day of this experiment and the day of our performance, as we all got ready, I think I changed boots three times. This was my first time fronting a band. And if you know me at all, you know that my personal edgy style was made for the stage. I have had short, spiky hair for years, usually dyed platinum blonde or some other fun shade. I may be soft spoken, but visually, I was made to stand out in the crowd and I was going to take full advantage of this once-in-a-lifetime opportunity to dress the part and properly front a rock band.

After much deliberation, I landed on a blood red, mostly backless halter top with loosely woven, beaded straps, black vegan leather leggings, and the safe but sexy booties. I wanted my outfit to be perfect for my moment in the spotlight. (I think focusing on my appearance was easier than facing what was about to happen.) The closer we got to showtime, the larger the butterflies in my stomach grew. They felt like they had actually turned into Pterodactyls by the time I was to walk on stage. And they took up so much room in my tight chest that there was no room for air to breathe. I was completely petrified. The place was packed. I thought for sure I would trip on the steep stairs leading up to the stage and completely forget my lyrics. As the last person in our band to make it on stage, I made my way up to my spot in front, and was somehow able to introduce myself and the band, in spite of the Pterodactyl beating down its large wings in my chest. And when I messed up the lyrics to one of our songs during our performance, I did not die. It is truly hard to believe, but I may have even had a teeny tiny bit of fun, as I sang our favorite original song, that I had a large part in writing. As I hissed, "Ssssnakes in Vegas" and enjoyed our fun, clever lyrics, I looked out onto the crowded dance floor and saw my friends who had come to support me, and I felt an immense wave of pride wash over me. I was truly 'doing the thing'.

Afterwards, I posted on Facebook, "This weekend I had one of the most exhilarating experiences of my life. I completed a big bucket list item of performing on stage in front of a large group of people, many of them complete strangers. I may not be the city's next undiscovered voice talent, but I sure had fun, and am so proud of myself and every other amazing woman that shared the experience with me!"

With all of my cliff jumping, and continual efforts, I have definitely gotten more comfortable taking up space. I still try to be succinct and sometimes struggle to take up space in group Zoom shares, but the fact that I 'raise my metaphorical hand' to speak up at all, is huge. And, I have gotten slightly better at, and more comfortable with, speaking in front of larger groups of people.

Speaking in front of a camera when I don't know who is on the other side still terrifies me. I believe in large part that this is because of the traumatic experience that I had in the courtroom at age thirteen, along with generations of trauma experienced by the women in my bloodlines around using our voices and taking up space, but I still show up and I do it anyway. And every single time I do, I feel proud of myself when I am done, because I know what it has taken to get me to this point.

I am still a work in progress. Maybe I will never be 100% comfortable speaking in front of a camera or an auditorium full of people, but I will die trying, because being someone who lives from my values of integrity, freedom, and growth is hugely important to me.

I have given so much thought over the years to what makes me different. What makes me different from my foster sisters? What makes me different from others that have been given every opportunity in life, and from those like me that have worked very hard for every opportunity? What makes me different from so many others I have come across in my life? What I have come up with is that it is something innate; my sheer determination and drive for growth and learning. This seeker quality in me is always pushing, always searching, and has me always striving to do better. It is what has led me to this journey of wanting to speak out and be more comfortable using my voice and allowing myself to be seen.

It is also what had me decide to take a huge leap of faith and start a nonprofit to empower women. It is what had me quit drinking, and join Toastmasters to attempt to get over my fear of public speaking. It is the force that pushes me through the fear every single time I choose to be on video for an event or a social media post.

I have learned that using my voice is part of my soul journey. I have learned that I have important things to say. I have spent a lifetime learning lessons that could benefit others and I am meant to share them. I have learned that my truth is my medicine and can be medicine for others, especially other women who might be on a similar journey and looking for inspiration or permission. I strive to be an example of what is possible and to lead the way. If I can stand fully in my power by using my voice, then you absolutely can too. There is nothing to be gained from being quiet or 'good', especially when it means dimming your own light. May your voice be strong and your purpose be clear. And may you be able to listen to the voice of your inner wisdom, so that you can know when it is time to speak out and use your unique voice and exercise your power in a way that makes a difference in our crazy, beautiful, mixed up world. After all, we are all in this together. And when one of us stands up and speaks out, it gives another permission to do the same, and we all win

> There is nothing to be gained from being quiet or 'good', especially when it means dimming your own light.

because we can truly see and connect with another human's experience, ultimately knowing that we are all far more alike than different, and that we are not alone.

Ivy Kaminsky

Ivy Kaminsky is a Self-Love and Light Whisperer committed to leading by example. She helps seekers and healers develop an unshakeable sense of self-worth and self-love, so they can show up, speak freely, and serve fully.

Ivy has a Master's degree in Development Studies from Kwa-Zulu Natal in South Africa and a Bachelor's degree in Communication Studies from the University of St. Thomas in St. Paul, Minnesota. She is a recent graduate of the Quantum Coaching Academy and is always learning, growing, and challenging herself in new and exciting ways.

In 2016, she started her own nonprofit empowering women. Ivy is a champion for women and loves to see them succeed, which explains why she would become a life coach helping women transform their lives and their relationships with their own worth, purpose, and power.

Ivy lives her values of integrity, growth, connectedness, freedom, and wellness and inspires others to do the same. Ivy's edgy, rock and roll outer appearance is juxtaposed with her inner calm, and her wise and loving demeanor. She rides a motorcycle and loves to travel any chance she gets. Ivy is passionate about all things women's empowerment, and Tarot and oracle cards.

CONNECT WITH IVY

 @elevatewithivy  linktr.ee/elevatewithivy

CHAPTER 2

Paris, PCOS, and the Pandemic:

MY UNLIKELY PATH TO PREGNANCY

By Simerjit (Sim) Sethi

The cab dropped us off and we pulled our suitcases over the cobblestone road which led us to an entrance that could've been mistaken for an alleyway. We climbed up the narrow spiral staircase and took in a deep breath, feeling accomplished and relieved.

We made it! We were in Paris! It was 2019 and we were so excited to be celebrating our 4 year wedding anniversary in such a romantic place.

We got dressed and left the hotel, excited to take in the sights, smells, and buttery croissants for the first time.

My mind was chaotic, weaving in and out of different scenarios, now that the thought of starting a family was a real possibility. I had finished my last pack of birth control after more than a decade of pumping my body full of it. It felt like such an abrupt ending to a long term relationship. A tiny little pill that I had been convinced was helping me for so many years, cut out of my routine just like that. The irony of feeling like I was so connected to my body for all those years—and the reality that it was just the false sense of control that kept me hooked—started to sink in.

As the trip progressed, I noticed myself having a more difficult time adjusting to the time zone compared to previous vacations. I lay in bed, wide awake in the middle of the night and dead tired in the middle of the day, pondering to myself whether this exhaustion was the jet lag, all the walking or…was I pregnant already? The faint possibility was exciting and also made me feel a bit nervous. Could it happen so quickly? Were we really ready for that huge life change? Would this be the last vacation we took before becoming a family?

Little did I know, this possibility would pop into my mind frequently over the next year—always ending in disappointment.

My husband had no idea that all these thoughts were swirling around in my head. At that point, being open and vulnerable about the amount of mental space this one topic took up felt embarrassing. We had talked about our desire to have a family many times at this point, always bouncing back and forth between the only two, very distinct options in our minds. Option one was to continue to live the jet setter life or option two "settle down."

This trip was unforgettable, leaving us dreaming of morning cappuccinos and croque monsieurs at the cafe around the corner. But the physical, mental, and emotional rollercoaster was something I thought I could leave in Europe.

Upon returning home, I downloaded a few period tracking apps to my phone, thinking this would help me build a deeper connection with my body. At the time, I thought killing myself at the gym, restricting calories, and trading in my evening treat for a cup of smooth camomile tea was going to solve all my problems.

But, nothing changed and I was actually feeling worse than ever before. Perhaps it was just the increased attention I was giving to my body. Perhaps it was the fact that all this effort I was putting in didn't seem to add up to how I was feeling. But, maybe it was just my body nudging me along to get to where I would end up just a few months later.

The math seemed simple—we were ready to start a family, my period cycles were all over the place, and I wasn't getting pregnant. So, the only option was to go against my intuition and see a fertility specialist, right?

● ● ●

As soon as I arrived the sterile environment was unavoidable. The way the paper crinkled underneath me, the way the gloves were stacked up on the counter, the smell of antiseptic—all made it impossible to forget where I was. Yet, this space had been created for the purpose of discussing something so sacred, so natural, so human. The clock was ticking and as each second went by, I was reminded that my biological clock was also ticking away. This was the day that I would find out my fate. It took months to convince myself to call the scheduler, to admit that I might need to be "fixed."

The air felt thick—almost as if it was a sign from nature that a predator was nearby. The door swung open so easily, as naturally as the wind blowing falling leaves away from a tree. As he walked in, I noticed that his hair was gelled perfectly, a crisp white coat hung from his broad shoulders, and he had a smile that deserved to be on posters.

"Hi, Mrs. Sethi?" He inquired.

I smiled.

"What can I do for you today?"

I took a breath, as if I was preparing for a gun to go off at a track race, and let it all out. I told him everything that led up to this point—the facts, my opinions, my family history, and previous information I had gathered from my gynecologist.

It appeared that he had perfected the act of making eye contact and nodding along while silently working out what time he needed to get out of the room to stay on schedule for the day.

He questioned each piece of my story, ignored my individual knowledge and the many years I had accrued living in my own body. It was almost as if he was trying to convince ME that nothing was even wrong. I didn't want anything to be wrong, yet I needed him to believe me in that moment. It felt as if we were playing a game of cat and mouse—but wait, who was prey?

I threw in some research with my next inquiry. There it was, the swift change in energy; it was now clear that I might have more insight than he originally thought. He looked back at the computer screen in silence, perhaps considering his attack plan. He moved through the motions, started to use more complex explanations and then stated he would conduct a vaginal ultrasound. He looked at the screen in silence. He moved the probe around and eventually removed it and asked me to sit up.

"I guess you could convince me," he replied after considering all the details.

I looked at him with confusion spread across my face.

"You could convince me that you meet the criteria to be diagnosed with PCOS (Polycystic Ovarian Syndrome)."

The diagnosis that I had convinced myself was not possible.

Sure, it ran in my family —but I was different. I was special.

I was better…at least that is what I had convinced myself.

A quick surge had me frozen, as if I was standing in a pile of snow. My body was doing the appropriate things—asking questions, nodding in agreement, getting dressed.

But, I couldn't get those words out of my head. "I guess you could convince me." *Where did we divert to the land of convincing?*, I thought to myself.

"I'll write you a script for letrozole, pick it up at CVS and you can speak to the front desk about getting scheduled for your first follow-up appointment on your way out. It was nice to meet you!" The words flowed out of his mouth as easily as a stream of melted water coming from the snow bank I felt I was standing in. As he edged toward the door, I snapped back into action. This medication was meant to force my body to ovulate. I knew that this was an option that is often prescribed to women with PCOS—without any further questions or exploration of what else could be going on.

"Okay, I understand that I have PCOS but from what I know, there are things I can do to reduce the symptoms." He stood still, blank faced—now he was frozen. "So…" I continued, "If I decide to take this medication to help me get pregnant, what can I do in the meantime to help with all my other symptoms?" It took me years of learning, reading, tracking, and working with specialists to formulate this very real, very honest question that I knew had an answer.

It was as if I had transformed into a creature from another land right in front of his face. "What do you mean?" he said.

"What if I want more kids and I want to feel better in the meantime?"

His shoulders relaxed and a smile crossed his face. "Oh! You just come back and we do this all again!"

This answer made sense when it came to growing a family. However, it ignored the exhaustion, sugar cravings, poor sleep, and aching body I was dealing with on a daily basis. Was this what life was all about? How could I thrive in motherhood if I was scraping by during the "best years" of my life? There had to be more. *There had to be another way*, I thought to myself.

This time he was too quick—the shocked part of me and the action part of me could not pair up quick enough. My mind had been wondering for too long and he was gone. On to the next patient.

I made my way to the front desk, feeling like the ticking clocks had stopped— everything around me was a blur as my mind kept racing and replaying the conversation in my head.

"Give us a call when you get your next period and we will set everything in motion!" said the scheduler with a big smile. I realized I had walked all the way back to the front of the office by this point.

I left feeling defeated and confused. I got an answer. I should be happy, right? The sense of defeat was amplified by a $500 bill that arrived shortly after that appointment. I would soon come to find out the feeling of confusion was simply my intuition reminding me that the outcome I felt so connected to was very much possible.

● ● ●

The juxtaposing feelings I was having over the next few months started to take on more of a personality. These battling voices in my head originated from what felt like two separate worlds that I somehow managed to be living in simulataneously. One character was very much connected to that sterile world. She felt familiar. After many years working as a provider in acute care hospitals, learning about the Western medical system, I thought her way was the only way. The research suggested that my difficulty getting pregnant was due to a hormonal imbalance, so "just take the medication to bypass the imbalance and you will get pregnant!" is what I often heard.

So, why did I still have so many questions? Plenty of people in this world had the beautiful outcome of expanding their family by going down this route. The even more confusing part was that I was so thankful for this option and the fact that so many children have come into the world because of modern medicine. I've always known that options are a sign of privilege.

However, the other character would not leave me alone. She kept urging me to trust my intuition, even though I was not sure where her path would lead me. I had no examples of the beautiful outcome of this alternative route. I had no idea of the timing. I had no real reason to trust this character—other than the deep, sacred, and natural connection we've had since before I was even born.

So there I was, stuck with two choices that both seemed to have the outcome that I desired. I think this might have been the first time that I really stepped back and realized that the journey might actually be more important than the outcome.

That was not what I had believed up until this point in life. I was more of a "put the work in and make it happen" kind of girl. Something in me knew that the masculine approach, the pushing and forcing, was not going to work this time. It was time I started to believe that I actually did know what was best for my own life, despite the lack of proof I felt I had. It was time I leaned into the allowing, the believing, the feminine approach. The problem was I had no idea where to start.

Starting a family was not a single person decision in my case. My husband and I had numerous conversations about what felt like the next right move for us. This might have been when I had another big reminder.

I happened to have married the person who was created for me.

The word supportive does not begin to describe what he provided me in these moments of doubt. It felt like my intuition jumped out of my body for a moment and was speaking through him. It was as if he was never even phased by the lack of proof we had to follow the path of the character that felt good, rather than the recommendations from the well-researched fertility specialist that sounded good. He encouraged me to simply be comfortable and confident with whatever choice I felt was right for my own body.

A couple of days after that dreaded appointment, I was changing for bed and I glanced over at the beautiful, silver full-length mirror that leaned up against the wall next to my dresser. This mirror was a generous wedding gift that had traveled with us since the start of our marriage. It had seen my reflection in our first little NYC one bedroom apartment as well as the version of me standing in the beautiful home we purchased in Philadelphia. The home we knew had extra room to welcome a little one into our world. This mirror had seen so many sides of me. The side of me in my late twenties, enjoying the city life as a career-driven woman with an alarm that reminded me to take my birth control, as not to ruin the "good years" of being free and jet setting around the world. This mirror saw the side of me entering into my thirties, putting on a pretty dress and a smile, as I prepared to go to celebrate what felt like every single friend moving forward into parenthood, while we remained as a couple. This mirror saw the recent version of me that would turn to the side, dreaming of the day that I would be excited and smiling seeing my growing belly, knowing that my body was creating a safe space to welcome the thing that would transition us from couple to family.

On this particular night, as the mirror reflected back my conflicted face, I started to think more and more about the different options that we had. I let the logical character take over for a moment. "You take care of your body, you feed it well, you work out, and you've been tracking your cycles. Maybe you need to accept the help." I pondered this idea for a moment. She made me question my choices. Was she right? Was I just being stubborn?

I welcomed the other character into the conversations for a moment. The one who was warm and calm. "Do what feels right, right now. You are always allowed to change your mind. Accepting help does not make you any less than. You can continue to follow your intuition and stop if something feels off." She made me feel good.

She reminded me that what we had were choices. And that was something to celebrate.

I decided to let that fact be my guiding light.

My husband and I decided to give the medication, letrozole, a chance. It was clear to me that the doctor I had seen was very interested in helping me get pregnant, but did not care too much about the bigger picture. I knew there was a way to get everything I wanted. As that warm and loving character taught me, I could always stop if I wanted to. I decided that I had nothing to lose and everything to gain.

The medication and monitoring could only be started at the beginning of a period cycle. So, I started another round of the very-frequently-played game of "when will my period come?" I waited…and waited… so that I could call the scheduler and get things started.

My frustrations increased as I waited multiple days past a "normal" cycle. As I reflect on this time, I can now see how God was clearly with me this month. This delayed period was very much on purpose—but that was before I really learned to trust that I was being given everything

I asked for.

It was March 16th, 2020. The day the city of Philadelphia went into lockdown. I naively picked up the phone to call the scheduler.

"Hi, I am calling to schedule my baseline ultrasound before starting Letrozole."

"Oh." She sounded disappointed.

"So, due to the COVID-19 pandemic we are suggesting that any new patients, who have not yet started treatment, wait to begin until we have a better idea how this will affect pregnant women. It should only be about 6 weeks, so just give us a call back around then."

"Oh…okay… thanks." I hung up feeling a bit confused. The two characters in my mind were battling over whether this was just going to delay the process of starting a family or if this was actually a good thing.

I didn't have too much time to play peacemaker for these two characters. The stress of the pandemic was on the rise and my fertility struggles would have to take a backseat for a bit. My responsibilities at work and home allowed me to escape the need to figure it all out for a moment. The desire for a family was still on my mind but the state of the world forced me to focus on all the things I was already blessed with in my life.

As luck would have it, my sister happened to reach out to me to tell me about a podcast she had come across. The host, Clare, was advertising a holistic protocol specifically for women with PCOS. I was intrigued. I had no idea something like this existed! I listened to a couple episodes of the podcast and found myself feeling even more interested.

That night, I washed my face and brushed my teeth, ready to settle in for the night. I got dressed for bed and glanced over in the mirror to see the reflection of a woman who felt excited and empowered by this new opportunity. I pulled the cool sheets over my body as I opened up my laptop. I sat on the bed looking at the information on the website and as I scrolled down to the bottom of the page I saw the "Get Started" button.

I took a breath, clicked the button, and saw that this program was twelve weeks long and the total price was just under $500. I felt an immediate ping of guilt. How could I spend even more money after that equally expensive bill from the fertility specialist?

My husband could see the conflict across my face and simply said, "It doesn't sound like you have anything to lose, we have to wait to go back to the doctor anyways, give it a try!"

That was all I needed, a moment of my intuition speaking through him once again. Pulling me from everything I had to lose and redirecting the focus on everything there was to gain from this gift of time we were being given. I signed up that night and started working through the daily content.

I was deeply inspired by this program—the level of support and the community that came along with it. For so long I chose to believe that I should just be able to figure things out on my own. The internet has endless information and there are so many free resources available. However, what I lacked to understand is that diving down the internet rabbit hole was simply adding to the guilt I already felt. It was making me feel worse about not being able to figure out the secret recipe to healing. What I also struggled to understand was that all of the free resources were not telling me what *my* body needed and why *I* was feeling worse than ever.

This program was the first time I heard of a "root cause approach." This simple idea means that when you treat the deeper issue—almost like feeding water and nutrients directly into the roots of a plant—the opportunity for success is significantly higher. I realized that up until this point, I was simply throwing things at the leaves of the plant and hoping they would get absorbed. The bonus of this program was how deeply supported I felt. It was as if the community that came along with this program was the soil that would offer a solid foundation for me to grow tall.

Before this program, I would pick up my phone and click the little red and white app, tracking my symptoms, not having much faith that this pre-coded program would be able to predict anything beneficial for me. I was used to the period tracking apps being just as confused as I was. They would follow the maze in my head that was always the same. It would begin with the idea that my period would start in two days, then two more days and then the hint that I might want to take a pregnancy test and eventually the disappointing end of the maze that resulted in a negative test and terrible cramps.

However, after just six weeks of following this new program, the magic was already brewing. My periods were becoming more regular, my sleep improved and my energy felt stable. I was so amazed by these results. Six weeks of supporting my body in the way it needed and so many things started to fall into place.

This was the feminine approach I had been searching for. I never realized that doing less was going to be the magic answer. It was during these six weeks that I really started to slow down. I went for walks instead of high intensity cardio, I ate what my body needed instead of restricting calories. I slept in more and I was taking vitamins and minerals that my body was lacking. The results felt immediate, even though I know in reality they were subtle.

●　●　●

This rapid change, paired with the frustration that I did not know all this information earlier, threw me down a path of deep diving into learning more about the root cause approach to health. That interest led me to sign up for a health coaching certification program where I learned even more about my body and how to support it for long term health.

It was during this awakening that I leaned further into my yoga practice, started meditating regularly, and made space in my life for massive mindset shifts to emerge. This required me to let go of everything I thought I once knew in order to have everything I really wanted.

That calm, supportive voice that has been with me since before I was born was so happy. It felt as if she was standing tall and proud seeing that I could finally notice where it was she was leading me all along. As I glanced in the mirror next to my dresser, I was reminded that the girl standing in front of me already knew all the answers. I was reminded that if I make time to connect to her and listen to her, she will never lead me down the wrong path. She reminded me that trusting my intuition is the most powerful thing I could ever do.

I continued to trust this voice and so many things changed over the next six months. I left my job as a Rehabilitation Director in the summer of 2020 and started an online business focused on health and mindset. I quickly became passionate about creating space for gentle transformation for women who desired the step by step process to implement sustainable changes in their lives, achieve their goals more easily, and to live the life they once dreamed of.

It was January of 2021, and this was the start of Sim Sethi Coaching and the launch of my first virtual group coaching program. With my husband working from home as well, we had an opportunity to grab our computers and go!

We arrived in Florida and tossed down our bags, glanced over at the beautiful view of the blue ocean rippling toward the coast and took in a breath of salty air.

As I walked around the pool, in my neon orange bikini, talking to my best friend on the phone, I told her how this was the first time in years that I felt truly comfortable in my own skin. Sure, I had lost a few pounds but I didn't look much different. One thing was different though. I was treating my body in a way that was healthy, supportive, and nourishing. This was a stark difference from the restriction, guilt, and punishment of the past. The choice to eat the salad over the fries may have looked the same from the outside. But those little choices were being guided by the character within me that only wanted the best for my life—not the one that was constantly judging and questioning me.

This trip might sound like a small and insignificant experience. However, being connected with my body, not overthinking every swimsuit, dinner outfit, and picture angle on this trip felt like the freedom I never knew was possible.

As I got changed for dinner I knew that the girl reflected back at me in the mirror when I arrived home was going to be so proud of this version of her.

●　●　●

The next year was a bit of a rollercoaster. The highest part of that ride was glancing down a few weeks after arriving home from Florida to see a positive pregnancy test on the morning of Valentine's Day. This was swiftly followed by a plummeting downhill turn of experiencing an early miscarriage, just a few weeks later.

It is easy to look back now, as I am getting off this ride, to see how each moment that followed was all very much on purpose. It is easy to see how the timing wasn't right for the life I was asking for.

But in that moment, the negative, judging character was back in my head trying to get me to question if I had made the right choices up until this moment. Here is the thing though, even on the hardest days, that voice could no longer win. The volume of that voice was turned down so low that it had become just a whisper in my mind that deserved no attention.

I always knew there was a purpose to the pain that I experienced during that miscarriage and I can see now how it cracked me open. I can see now how the darkest cracks are where the brightest light has the chance to enter.

There were many moments during that year that I would walk by my beautiful silver trimmed mirror and see a version of my life reflected back that I didn't want. This was not how it was supposed to go. This timeline didn't follow the plan I created when I was 22 and mapped out when each big moment would take place. But I couldn't avoid that mirror. It was in my face the moment I woke up each day and it was reflecting back my reality each night when I got ready for bed. I'm sure there was a moment that I can no longer recall when I decided to surrender and to start allowing that mirror to reflect back exactly what my life looked like. Somewhere in there, I also decided to enjoy it, exactly as it looked.

2021 was a year filled with deep yet gentle transformation. The heartache and hope created opportunities for depth in my marriage and relationships. It forced me to allow support in a way I had never allowed in my life. It showed me how I was able to show up even more powerfully for my own clients by being willing to let others show up for me. These were lessons I never wanted to learn, but I quickly realized that my existence would be less meaningful and less impactful without them. It was all part of the plan.

● ● ●

Daylight peeked in through the window on the morning of Valentine's Day at the beginning of 2022. It was a Monday morning and my heart was racing, but it wasn't the rush of the alarm on this particular day. The distraction of a busy day filled with responsibilities was exactly what I needed. I pulled myself out of bed, brushed my teeth and got dressed as my heart continued pounding. As the day progressed, I became more and more distracted. I found myself wandering around just to realize I was already walking in the direction I needed to go. I sat down for a moment to take in a deep breath, a long exhale, and a sip of water.

As I glanced down at the calendar on my phone, I reflected back on this day, exactly one year ago. I reflected back on the joy I felt as I looked at that positive pregnancy test with disbelief. I reflected back on the joy I felt that day—thinking that everything had finally paid off.

Within an instant, I was jolted back to reality by a construction vehicle passing outside the window. I was jolted back to the joy and sorrow of my current situation. My coaching career was going better than I imagined, the freedom I always desired was now my reality, and I felt so deeply connected to my body. This was balanced out by the emptiness I felt going into my home office, which was meant to be a nursery, arriving to events as a couple when we longed to be a family and fielding constant questions about whether we wanted kids or not.

These conflicting feelings were elevated by the fact that my period was late. I chalked it up to the stress that had been building up over the last few weeks as we approached this "anniversary." I finished up my day, feeling just as distracted as when it started, and headed upstairs to shower.

I peeled off my clothes from the day, ready to get into the shower, but something stopped me. There was something I needed to do before we left for another trip to Florida the next day.

I stood in front of the tiny bathroom window admiring the shades of orange and purple as the sun was setting. The feel of the cold tile floor under my toes reminded me that I wasn't floating. I set it down and found myself sitting on the plush gray bath mat just in front of the glass shower door. I closed my eyes—feeling the air entering into my nose and leaving my lungs just as quickly.

How could three minutes possibly take this long? I thought.

I closed my eyes again—focusing on my breath. That's when I heard it—the faint whisper, as if something or someone was leaning down from the sky to let me know "everything is about to change." I glanced down at my watch… finally! Three minutes was up. I stood up—walked over to the counter and my jaw dropped.

My heart was racing and tears filled my eyes—could I really trust it this time? The pregnancy test said positive, but after so many negative tests, I felt I couldn't trust this little device that you can buy for a couple bucks at CVS. Then I remembered the message I had just received: "Everything is about to change."

Then I remembered the message I had just received:

"Everything is about to change."

I was pregnant.

Me, the girl who was told that the only way was with medications and special pills. But I did it, on my terms, my way, and on the timeline that was meant for me. This was the story I had been waiting to tell. The story I had visualized so many times. But that day, the story transformed from fiction to fact.

As the weeks progressed, each appointment, blood-draw-and-nausea-filled day, served as a reminder that the voice I heard sitting in the bathroom that evening was telling the truth.

There was also a part of me that really struggled with some anger in those early weeks of pregnancy. I was mad that the joy of pregnancy had been sucked out of me after experiencing a miscarriage. I was tired of constantly feeling worried and scared. I was frustrated that each appointment made me feel like I was holding my breath—placing all of my energy into something I could not control.

So, I decided to reclaim my joy.

I am not saying this was immediate or even easy—but it was so worth it. I decided to accept and trust that everything *was* about to change. I decided to celebrate every single day of this pregnancy. I decided to spend my time connecting to this beautiful soul that chose me.

* * *

As I glance in the tall, beautiful silver mirror today, I see a girl who followed her intuition. I see a girl who was brave enough to trust herself. I see a girl who decided what she wanted and believed it was possible. I see a girl who stopped thinking she had to do it alone. I see a girl who accepted help. I see a girl who trusted that everything she desired was on the way—even if it looked different than she imagined.

And, underneath the hand that rests on my growing belly, I feel the gentle movement of a little girl who will soon know that all of this is possible for her, too.

Simerijt (Sim) Sethi

Simerjit (Sim) Sethi is a passionate Health & Mindset Coach, Adjunct Professor, Author and Speech-Language Pathologist who is dedicated to helping people live a life of peace and adventure.

Her time in NYC left her with a Master's in Communicative Sciences and Disorders from NYU and the belief that you CAN have anything in this life you desire.

She has been passionate about the health and wellbeing of people her whole life. It is this passion which led her to work in healthcare for ten years, before following her intuition and starting a Health & Mindset Coaching business.

Since 2020, Sim has led hundreds of people through group experiences, coaching programs and 1:1 sessions, while using the many modalities she is trained in, to bring individuals into a deeper relationship with themselves. Her ultimate goal is to offer a space for gentle transformation within a safe community.

When Sim is not coaching, teaching, or working at the hospital you can find her planning her next trip, reading a good book on the beach, or concocting a new meal with whatever she can find in the fridge!

CONNECT WITH SIM

 @sim_sethi_coaching    linktr.ee/sim_sethi

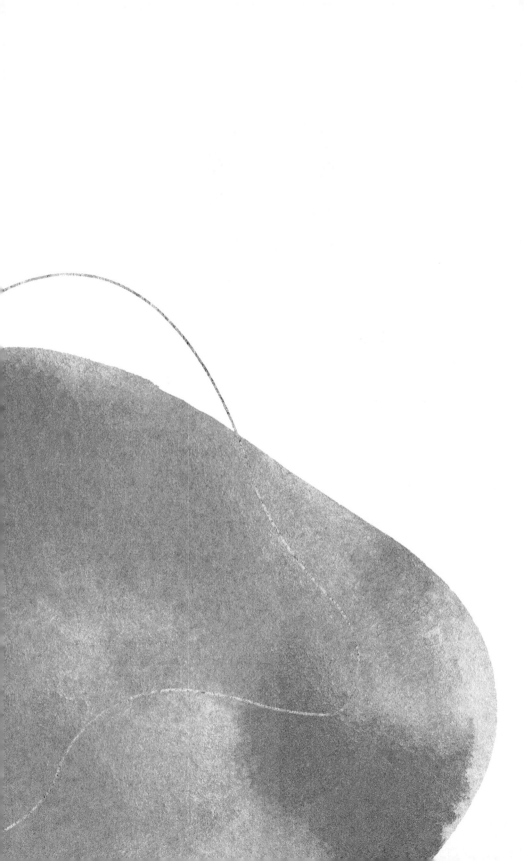

CHAPTER 3

From Shame to Sparkle:

RISING FROM THE RUINS OF TOXIC RELATIONSHIPS

By Jennifer Wreyford

The TSA agent looked from my ID to his wristwatch, then up at my tear-stained face.

"Miss Jennifer…it's officially your birthday, there should be no tears!"

"I…I know, sir, thank you…."

He handed back my ID.

"You ok, Miss Jennifer?"

"Yes, sir…I….it's just been a…it's been…a really bad night"

"Alright then," he said, waving me through. "Happy Birthday."

His kindness, in the face of the cruelty I'd just experienced, brought a fresh wave of tears bubbling up through my chest and threatening to unleash an audible sob. Fighting hard to hold it in, I nodded a vigorous thank you and moved forward to the empty screening lane.

I'd been thirty-seven for less than three hours, in the city of neon and noise. Now there was only the sound of my own footsteps and suitcase wheels, echoing through the strange, empty vastness of a place usually bustling with people.

I tucked myself into a seat at the end of a row in the sea of empty chairs, hugging my knees to my chest. It was too early to call my best friend, though it hadn't stopped me from making a frantic, tearful phone call to my mother from the Vegas hotel room. My mind wound back to sobbing into the phone to my mom, as I threw clothes wildly into my suitcase with my other hand. "Mom, he tricked me, this trip was all a lie!" I wailed.

Instead of an overnight romantic birthday getaway, my boyfriend had gifted me an elaborate ruse, a midnight breakup, and a $1,200 hotel bill (a lovely addition to my mountain of credit card debt). This crazy plot twist had been meticulously planned to exact "revenge" for "wrongs" he'd created out of thin air, along with supporting "evidence" so ridiculous it would never stand up in court.

What a mess. I glanced at the time. The first flight home wasn't until 6am. There would be no sleeping, that much I knew. Nothing was open. I couldn't even get a cup of coffee to comfort me as I waited. Too many hours to kill with nothing but the jarring memories of the last few hours to keep me company. I closed my eyes and let them wash over me.

● ● ●

The trip itself should have been my first clue something was off. Sad as it was, he'd never offered to take me anywhere special and he'd sure never given a damn about my birthday. He would often tell me birthdays only mattered to me because I was an only child, and no one else really cared. A sudden birthday trip to Vegas should have set off alarm bells, but I wanted to believe the best.

My intuition pinged in the taxi to the hotel, when he casually mentioned we needed to use my credit card for the trip. He made an excuse about his CFO asking him to stop using his card until they sorted something out. It didn't make sense, but who was I to question him? I didn't run a multimillion-dollar business and I was painfully insecure about my ignorance of how such things worked, so I said of course it would be fine. He assured me he would pay me back, and I had no reason to doubt him, right?

Then, as I was getting ready for dinner, there was the weird text from an unknown number—just "Happy Birthday" with a photo of a building two blocks from my apartment. I replied, "Thank you, but who is this?" No response.

His infidelity had turned me into quite the detective, so I did a reverse Google search for the number. I stared in confusion as I read the entry my search had returned. The phone traced back to my boyfriend's CFO. Strange, sure, but I still didn't think it was anything sinister. I remember thinking, still so lost in delusion, that it must be part of a birthday surprise. Maybe he'd bought a condo in that building, since he knew how much I loved the neighborhood. What else could explain the photo? It never crossed my mind that it could be something awful. I went back to primping for Vegas birthday fun, deciding he must have an elaborate surprise planned.

And did he ever.

As our night crept closer to midnight, he started announcing a countdown.

"An hour to your birthday," he said as we left the Cirque show.

"Half hour to your birthday," he said, as he taught me how to play craps.

Wow, he's really taking this birthday thing seriously this time, I thought.

"Ten minutes to your birthday," he said. "Let's go upstairs and regroup before we go back out."

I felt impressed, touched even, by how seriously he was taking my celebration. He had really listened to me this time and was really making an effort to show how much he cared.

Exactly at midnight, he got up from where he'd been sitting in our room and walked to the hotel safe, saying he had a present for me. *Was it jewelry?*, I wondered. *What else would you put in the safe?*

He plopped some things on the bed saying "Happy Birthday" again, this time with a vicious tone. He told me he was "on to me" that he had "all the evidence" he needed, that I'd be paying for this whole trip, that he'd done all of this to "ruin" my birthday because it was "exactly what I deserved."

What the hell was happening? What was he even saying? I'd had enough celebratory wine that my brain was struggling to put the pieces together. I looked at the collection of items on the bed. I was usually a quick thinker but I couldn't figure this one out.

A paper printout.

A Ziploc bag containing some gauzy scarves and a pair of flimsy toy handcuffs.

The bag…that was…wait, that was mine. I'd moved it at least ten times over the years, pack rat that I was. But it belonged in a drawer under my bed. *Why did he have it? And why was it here in Vegas?*

I reached for the paper, still confused. It was a printout of a screenshot from Find My Friends, with a building circled. The same building from the photo I'd received earlier in the cryptic text message. The building where my shitty cell phone reception kept placing my location, even though I'd never set foot inside it in my life.

He declared I'd been "having an affair with a man" there and that's why he'd called me at 3am a few nights before—to see where I was. "Where I was" had been in my own bed next to a girlfriend who was visiting for a weekend yoga retreat, very much asleep and very much annoyed at his phone call. I told him as much. He snarled that I had lied and that she'd lied for me too, "of course." She'd been my "alibi" because those were "the kinds of friends" I had. "Liars," he said, just like me.

And the bag of scarves with the toy cuffs? According to him, those were proof I was a whore who was into bondage, with an endless stream of men trouncing through my bedroom—nevermind that he could have come over to my apartment anytime to disprove his crazy theories. I was rapidly realizing logic and reason had exited stage left a long time ago.

I was willing to own the things I had done, but this? *This wild piece of slanderous fiction? Was I in the Twilight Zone? What was he even saying?* It wasn't the first time he'd led me to question what I knew to be reality. Much later, I'd learn there was a term for what I'd been experiencing, taken from an old Ingrid Bergman movie. All of this felt like a movie too, and a bad one.

After two years of his lies, deceptions, misdirections, infidelity, the hypocrisy of it all…how dare he…

Something broke loose deep inside of me.

I leapt off the bed fueled by unadulterated, animalistic rage. I hurled a heavy water bottle at his head, my normally excellent aim impaired by fury and wine, thankfully missing him by a mile. I yelled every horrible thing I could think of at him, what a hypocritical lunatic he was.

I screamed that I hoped he died.

Minutes later, my voice now raw and hoarse, I started packing frantically, making the call to my mom somewhere in between.

Before I slammed the door to the hotel room, suitcase in hand, I had enough clarity to know there was one thing I would regret no matter how much of a monster he'd been to me. I told him nothing excused what he'd done, that he was a hateful, miserable human being, but that I was sorry for telling him I hoped he died.

And that I never wanted to see him again.

Now I was sitting in an empty airport, alone on my birthday, the wee hours of the Vegas morning ticking quietly away toward sunrise. Snapping back to my body in the airport seat, I shook my head violently back and forth, in part to clear the memories and equally praying it would wake me up from this nightmare.

I exhaled heavily, my face still wet with tears.

How the hell had I gotten here?

How the hell had I gotten here? How had I let it all get so bad? I thought back to where it all began.

How had I let it all get so bad?

● ● ●

I'd met him on an airplane two years before, a few months after I left my second husband. His alcoholism had ruined our marriage and forced me into another divorce. I was adamant with my therapist that I was "totally fine" and it "hadn't been traumatic," never mind a police report to the contrary. I'd always thought your husband was meant to be your protector and your home meant to be a haven from the harsh world outside. I'd had to leave both for my own safety. That was the only thing that had been clear—having to leave. The rest was a jumble of shock, confusion, and heartbreak. Everything had been ripped away from me by his addiction, and I was desperately trying to run through the pain of losing my marriage to forces outside my control.

I wasn't even close to processing everything I'd been through in the past year. I was strong but broken, powerful yet barely pieced together. I didn't know what to do with the shattered pieces of my life—the one I'd so carefully and intentionally rebuilt once before.

What I did know was that I needed to get away. So I was flying to meet a girlfriend for a yoga retreat in Central America, hoping to find my footing again or at least a measure of peace.

I'd gifted myself a first class seat for my adventure, and buried myself in a book right after boarding. I paid little attention when an older gentleman settled into 2B next to me. Having resigned myself to living the rest of my days with only four-legged furry companions, I was polite but reserved when he struck up a conversation. He asked my destination, casually dropping in that he was a real estate developer and businessman in Costa Rica. *You're a hot shot, I get it. I'm not a dewy-eyed schoolgirl, sir, not interested*, I thought, as I nodded politely and went back to my book. I instantly categorized him as every stereotype I had about older, affluent men: likely married, likely unfaithful, and definitely not what I needed in my life.

My reticence to fall for his Southern charm must have intrigued him. Over the course of the flight he continued to engage me in conversation, gently resting a finger on my knee periodically as he talked. As we deplaned, he handed me his card and said, "Let me know how the retreat was, I'm always looking for places to refer people when they visit." I tucked it into my bag, wished him a good night, and made my way out of the airport where my friend was waiting by the curb to start our adventure.

"How was your flight?" she asked as I slid into the passenger seat of our rental.

"Oh, fine. I think some old dude was hitting on me. He was probably just being nice."

Even through the thick Costa Rican night, I could see her eyebrow arch.

"And I thought I was naive," she said, as she pulled out onto the main road.

I doubt I'd have thought twice about him after that, if we hadn't run into him the next day as we were leaving a beach bar. I happily exclaimed his name when I recognized him because when you're in a foreign country, any familiar face becomes a friend. He smiled broadly and offered to buy us a drink. We had a long drive ahead, so I declined and thanked him. He wished us safe travels and swaggered away. I journaled that night about our first full day of adventure and noted: *Ran into the guy I sat next to on the plane...proud to say I know one person now in Costa Rica.*

In spite of myself, that synchronicity was enough to spark girlish fantasies of a mystery man turned shining knight who would carry me off into a happy ending, a reward for everything I'd been through.

I sent him an email when I returned home, telling him what a beautiful country he'd chosen as a second home. After a few polite exchanges, flirtations crept in. A dinner invite followed the next time I was in his city. Despite the difference in our ages, we had more in common than I would have thought, and I really came to enjoy our conversations. He began courting me like the Southern gentleman he'd purported to be. I found myself swept away by it all and, in spite of my previous declarations that I'd be single forever, I fell fast for this charming man. I tied a blindfold over my eyes and dove, hard and head-first, into him. I was sure he would rescue me, protect me, be my salvation, my happy ending. I made him my life raft in my sea of pain, not understanding how vulnerable I was or that I was about to be tangled in a web of destructive trauma bonding.

* * *

A year into our relationship, I had become accustomed to waking up feeling queasy. The tightness in my chest had become so normal, I hardly noticed it anymore.

I chastised myself, again and again, for being unfair to him in my suspicions, for silently questioning everything he said and did.

My anxiety, my worry that he was hiding something…it had to be a tragic echo from my ex's alcoholism and all the lies I uncovered at the end.

That must be it.

He shouldn't have to pay for my past, I would tell myself over and over. I was barely functioning, I was so crippled by anxiety.

My doctor had increased my anxiety medication, but it was still getting worse with each passing day. A thousand flutters, contractions, and intuitive nudges told me something was wrong. Always explained away, always a plausible reason. Always thinking it was my fault, blaming myself for thinking the worst. Still, I couldn't shake that something… just wasn't right.

Then, on my thirty-sixth birthday, exactly one year before the fateful Vegas trip, his carefully constructed web of lies began to come to light. That was the first time I caught the "I love you" message out of the corner of my eye. He'd asked me to help him with his computer (his ignorance of modern technology would often prove his downfall), and there it was—an iMessage from a Costa Rican woman I'd met once on a trip with him. His explanation?

"It's for work, it's nothing. She's Latina, she's just very passionate and expressive about everything."

He then showed me just enough of their email correspondences to almost explain it away. If he was willing to do that, surely he couldn't be hiding anything, right? Without concrete proof, I told myself I didn't have a leg to stand on with my accusations.

The morning after that, he took his dog downstairs leaving his phone on the charger by the bed. When it rang at 6am, I glanced over and froze. It was the same woman from the iMessage. I fought my instinct to answer and find out what was really going on. But I told myself I couldn't be the crazy girlfriend answering his phone calls if it really WAS work.

A few weeks later, though, I had my chance. He was back from a trip to Bali, and exhausted from jet lag. He handed me his phone, asked me to fix something for him, and promptly passed out next to me on the couch.

With his phone unlocked in my hand and him snoring quietly beside me, I was free to roam his digital world.

This was not the time for discretion or blind trust. It was my opportunity.

I clicked on the green message bubble.

I didn't have to scroll far.

Ice flooded my veins. My stomach turned to pure black acid when I saw an all-too-personal "I miss you, handsome" message. It wasn't from me. I kept scrolling through message after message, all mutually professing love and clear sexual intimacy—many at the exact same time he'd been messaging me.

But it wasn't the same woman from the message and the phone call this time—it was a name I didn't recognize. *How many other women were there exactly??*

I clicked on the contact record. The ice in my veins froze even colder and my stomach hollowed out. The email address listed proved it was the same woman who had been calling and messaging him.

That fucker. He'd changed the display name of her contact record so I wouldn't notice her messages anymore.

I got up from the couch, shaking with pure rage and emotion, my breathing shallow and rapid. He stirred on the couch, but didn't wake.

I looked at him, wanting to vomit or kick him or both. Instead, I walked into the bathroom, his phone still in my hand. I steadied my breathing as I closed the door.

I looked in the mirror.

The woman who stared back at me had known the truth all along.

My body had been screaming at me for months to listen to what my brain, my heart refused to accept.

You knew. You just didn't trust yourself, I whispered to the woman in the mirror.

The ice in my veins suddenly thawed, as a wave of warm release rushed through me.

The tightness in my chest burst apart and I could breathe again.

Even in the midst of the pain of the betrayal, there was relief.

Relief in knowing I wasn't crazy.

Relief in remembering my intuition had never let me down…I'd just grown masterful at ignoring it.

I took a deep breath, put my hand on the doorknob, and stepped out to confront him with the truth.

● ● ●

Caught red-handed with irrefutable proof of his cheating, he swore up and down that it "only happened once." She was obsessed with him after it happened, he said, and he didn't know how to break contact with her because of the business connection. Then and there, I should have left his ass. One and done, no second chances. But I didn't. Instead, I told him I needed a few days to think.

That night, I found the other woman through Facebook and sent her a message. "I know about you and my boyfriend," I said. "He's not being fair to either one of us, but please, leave him alone."

A few days later, I received a message back: "Can we talk on the phone?"

There is no greater nightmare for a cheater than the two women he's been duping comparing notes and timelines. They'd been dating—she, too, thought exclusively—for nine months. Turns out she remembered me too, except he'd told her we'd broken up, that I was obsessed with him, stalking him, and he didn't know how to make me go away. *Hmm, seemed a common refrain.*

When I confronted him with proof of each and every lie he'd told to me and to her, I was surprised that he didn't make excuses, defend, or deflect. If he had tried to defend himself, maybe I would have left. I'll never know. But he seemed to take so much ownership of his behavior that it caught me off guard.

Through tears, he spun a story of how truly sorry he was, how much he cared for me, how he'd just gotten in so deep he hadn't known how to get out, how he didn't want to lose me so he kept lying, how he'd never do it again. Even through hurt, my heart went out to what seemed like true accountability. *Hadn't I found myself lost and confused before too? Didn't everyone deserve another chance to do better?*

I so deeply wanted to believe the best in him, trusting he would "do the right thing" once he received my grace and forgiveness. I had yet to learn that you can forgive someone and still keep them at a distance for who they've shown themselves to be. I also didn't want to "fail" in another relationship, so I was willing to swallow what he was serving up at the expense of my own self value.

That night, I made my first truly fatal mistake since I'd met him— one that would cost me in immeasurable ways for years to come: I told him I forgave him, and I took him back on the spot. I remember the look of shock on his face when I said it.

I also told a lie that night: I told him that if he ever did it again, I would leave. I was convinced he'd learned a lesson and would be reformed by my act of grace alone.

Instead, what he learned was that he could do anything he wanted to me with no natural consequences for his months of betrayal and deception. What he learned was that I was a doormat with no boundaries who could be treated like trash and continue to take it.

So I spent the next few months sick all over again, while he secretly rekindled a relationship with the other woman—a repeating cycle she and I would play out for far longer than either of us would care to admit. And when I caught him again, I broke my own word: I didn't leave. Every time I would catch him talking to her again, he'd dismiss me and I'd allow it. I'd cry, I'd feel horrible, I'd yell at him…but I stayed.

Instead of leaving, I let it eat me alive, destroying me slowly from the inside out until on yet another airplane in yet another first class cabin, I met a man who was incredibly kind and took a genuine interest in me. We started talking and texting. He became my water in the desert, the cool breeze reminding me maybe I was still valuable after all. It was such a relief to feel wanted and cared for that I had a six-week affair of my own, simultaneously happy to finally have a kind man's attention and equally consumed by guilt for my actions. I didn't even recognize myself anymore; I felt so damn lost and disconnected. I just wanted to numb everything I was feeling. So while I knew firsthand how destructive alcohol could be, I tried to escape my pain by drinking…a lot.

When my boyfriend finally caught me, he became the externalized voice of the worst things I'd ever thought about myself, which he shared frequently and loudly. Shame is insidious and leaves you vulnerable to abuse if it becomes your master. And I was eaten up with shame, both for the way I'd devalued myself in taking him back after his repeated lies and equally for my lack of integrity in having an affair. So I accepted every horrible, awful thing he said to me and every way he harassed me because I thought I deserved it as punishment.

I still didn't fully understand the extent of the backlash possible when an ego like his experienced an "injury," or that there was actually a term for it. His hypocrisy and disproportionate reaction to my indiscretion should have been another sign to me. There was no reasoning with him. None. The simplest analogy I can make for those who I hope never have to experience it firsthand is this:

Your partner walks into the kitchen, grabs the overflowing trash can, turns it upside down and smears it all over the kitchen. In your shock, you turn from cleaning the coffee maker and drop coffee grounds on the floor. Your partner then spends the next three hours berating you for what YOU did and how it's actually YOUR fault they turned that trash can upside down. In fact, you MADE them do it because of what you said or didn't say or what you did or didn't do. You're left feeling bewildered, questioning your grasp on what's real.

Needless to say, I had definitely gotten his attention and he was giving me LOTS of it now. Even if it was negative and abusive, some wounded and confused part of me felt satisfied to finally be taking up space in his life. My perception at this point was about as out of whack as it was possible to be.

In a calm moment between his raging storms, he claimed he loved me (something he'd never said before). He professed to me that this had all shown him how much he wanted to be with me, and how willing he was to work on this now. Yet again, I swallowed this as true because it was what I wanted to hear. I'd wanted so badly for my ex-husband to fight for our marriage, to fight through his addiction, to choose ME, and to choose US. That feeling was lingering in me like a cancer—the intense longing to have someone fight for me and for our relationship. *Wasn't that what was finally happening?*

Overnight, he did seem to change. Suddenly, the man who had kept me at a distance for years never wanted us to be apart. Suddenly, he wanted us to move to Costa Rica together and start a life. Suddenly, he was talking about marriage and shopping for three-carat diamond rings. And for a while, it almost seemed real. Wasn't this sudden obsession with me just my boyfriend finally showing he actually cared? Some part of me, the wiser part that I had buried deep down, knew something was wildly off and tried to send me signals that I continued to ignore. Every now and then, usually in a wine-induced haze, I'd have moments of clarity followed by anger at his bizarre double standards around infidelity. My inner voice was screaming at me to wake the fuck up this time and see this wasn't real, but I'd gotten too good at blocking it out.

A few months later, I would be on a plane with him to Vegas for a romantic birthday getaway—with no inkling of what was about to happen.

● ● ●

I would love to say I flew home from Vegas and never saw him again. I wasn't that strong yet. I was still bleeding from gaping wounds of unworthiness and shame, trapped in thinking the intensity and drama I had with this man was "love."

While Vegas did mark the beginning of the end, things would get much worse before they started to get better. As horrible as that trip had been, I was still falling through the abyss and hadn't hit rock bottom yet. I stayed locked in a toxic karmic battle with him for another two years while I slowly healed and grew through my own spiritual journey.

A few months after the infamous birthday trip, I finally blocked communication with him. But the following February, I ran into him on, ironically, a flight to Vegas. (For the record, I never go to Vegas anymore.) We would rekindle our dramatic Lifetime movie all over again because even though I had started my healing journey, I wasn't yet ready to see how toxic the relationship was. I endured more lies, more deceptions, and, this time, threats to ruin or humiliate me by leveraging his vast monetary resources and powerful connections against me.

And yet I still believed it could be different if I just tried hard enough. I was the perfect performing poodle, jumping through hoops to keep the peace, twisting myself into a pretzel to make it work, constantly making a case to him for how things could be better. For a time, it did seem to get better but relatively speaking that wasn't saying much. The core was still poisoned and rotten.

All the while, I continued to work on myself. I dove deep into healing and read everything I could get my hands on. I worked with energy healers, began meditating, and deepened in my yoga practice. And since my deepest pains had always been in romance, I became a student of relationships, of masculine and feminine energies, and of how unhealed patterns can manifest in a relationship—as well as how to work through them. It was all supporting my journey, and my heart was healing from decades of pain and unworthiness.

One decision during that time had the biggest impact: I hired an expert relationship coach who had a masterful and deep understanding of heart healing as well the dynamics between masculine and feminine. I began to have powerful realizations that were like bombs going off, blasting me awake.

She took my hand and lovingly guided me through every room within myself that I had been too scared to enter before. In each room where there had once been darkness, she would flip on the light and I'd be flooded with insights. She would gently help me see my own patterns and give support in healing them. Through our work, a part of me began to deeply recognize this relationship was the last thing I needed.

I remember the day she lovingly but firmly told me that I would soon have a choice to make: leave or stay. That it was a decision only I could make, and that one path would mean life…the other would mean accepting continual self-abandonment.

"Life or soul-death, Jen. It's ultimately your choice."

Her words landed in me like a gut punch. Immediately, I could feel their resonant truth. Every minute I stayed was eroding my soul. It truly was my choice to leave…or to stay. In the core of my being, I knew my answer. Yet I was scared to act on it because of what had happened the last time we'd broken up. I couldn't endure being terrorized and bullied again. I didn't know what would happen if I ended things with him this time.

Then one night, I was just ready.

There was no pivotal moment. It wasn't anything he did or said. I'd just grown enough in my consciousness to realize I didn't want to live this way anymore and I'd pay whatever price I had to pay to get out.

I lay in bed that night, staring at the ceiling, and I said aloud to the Universe:

"If it's meant to end, let it end, and let it be easy."

And when you finally declare to the Universe that—energetically, emotionally, mentally, physically—you're really ready? Well, that's when magic happens.

A few days later, he concocted yet another wild story that I was cheating, this time with my dog trainer (I wasn't), and stonewalled me for four days.

But this time was different.

I was done being accused and punished for something I didn't do.

Done being the shock absorber for his self-loathing and unprocessed pain.

Done being blamed for the ghosts of every lie he'd ever told to a woman to hide his own indiscretions.

I was DONE.

I was in full integrity with myself and ready to choose ME, no matter what.

So this time, I broke the pattern.

This time, I set REAL boundaries.

> I was in full integrity with myself and ready to choose ME, no matter what.

And two weeks after I pleaded with the Universe for an easy ending, that man got up off my couch and walked out of my life forever.

And this time, I let him go.

●　●　●

It would be easy to paint him as the villain and me as the victim. Except it's not true. There is no clear villain or singular victim here. In consideration of recounting a story that involves another human being,

I want to acknowledge here that there are moments in all our lives of which we aren't proud. Nothing excuses his actions, yet those actions continued because I continued to feed them. We were two people with varying degrees of wounding, coping mechanisms, and levels of consciousness with a destructive trauma bond between us.

He was toxic—but so was I. I was in a toxic cycle of unworthiness, self-abandonment, and codependency. And when you find yourself locked in a toxic relationship, it can be a hard pill to swallow to realize you are equally toxic in the dynamic—your toxicity just expresses itself differently than theirs. It means there is healing needed within you.

This is why the best way to guard against toxic relationships is to do your inner work to heal yourself, to learn what it means to love and accept all parts of yourself just as you are, to set real boundaries, and to stop your own cycles of self-abandonment once and for all.

If you recognize yourself in my story, I want to offer you some guideposts to start your journey.

- **Stop tolerating poor treatment and calling it "love."** Real love is NEVER abusive, punishing, or deceitful. Healthy relationships have disagreements. Sometimes, because we're human, we will say things that hurt our partner. The difference is that in a healthy relationship, you have a core of respect. You both seek to listen and to understand each other AND yourself so you can grow together and build a rock solid relationship foundation.

- **Stop listening to the voice in your head that says you'll "never find anyone better."** Even if it doesn't feel true yet, believe in advance that you're worthy and deserving of a healthy relationship. And if you aren't sure what a healthy relationship looks like, start by knowing you deserve to learn.

- **Stop saying you're "an empath" when what you really are is a doormat.** There is no Martyr Medal for "who can tolerate the most toxic person" (I've done the field research on this one). That is your own toxicity showing. You can understand their poison AND choose not to drink it yourself. In fact, you can be <u>incredibly</u> empathic and compassionate AND still hold strong ass boundaries to keep them at arm's length or remove them from your life entirely. Stop setting yourself on fire to keep someone else warm.

- **Start believing you're worthy of boundaries.** Simply put: we protect what we value. When you don't value yourself, you won't protect your time, your energy, your body, your spirit. You are worth setting boundaries for. Start to learn what yours are, how to set them, and what to do when someone crosses them. You do not need anyone's permission to set boundaries and you don't need to defend them to an invisible committee for them to be valid. They're your boundaries—that's all the validity you need.

- **Start getting support.** Find a coach, a mentor, a therapist, or a healer (or several!) who has been on the journey you're walking and successfully come through the other side. They can help you dramatically shorten the healing and learning process and quantum leap through what could take you years on your own. Always use your discernment as to who will be the right fit to guide you to heal and grow as the sovereign being you are.

And as always, remember:
Life's too short not to sparkle! Sparkle On...

Jennifer Wreyford

Jennifer Wreyford is the Founder and CEO (Chief Empowerment Officer) of Courage to Rise, a company born of her passion for leading others to an easier and more fulfilling life. She is also the creator of the 'Courage to Rise Method', a proprietary transformational program designed to give her clients the foundation and tools for truly lasting fulfillment in every area of life.

She's powered by coffee, humor, and a deep belief that healing the wound of unworthiness within each of us is the key to better relationships and a happier, healthier world. Jennifer sparkles, she cusses, and she serves up practical steps, compassionate guidance, and tough love when needed to help her clients get lasting results. She's also freakishly good at Ms. Pac-Man.

Jennifer lives in Denver, Colorado with her 18lb cat, Marlowe, and her 12lb dog, Spike. She'd appreciate it if you didn't report to the state of Colorado that she doesn't ski, cycle, or participate in '420.'

CONNECT WITH JENNIFER

@iamjenniferwreyford   jenniferwreyford.com

CHAPTER 4

Into the Light

By Amanda Goolsby

The light. The light was so bright, it was blinding.

It overcame my visual perception with so much intensity. I couldn't see my hands, my body, or anything of form. Just oneness, wholeness, infinite love. As I stood enveloped in the white light, I heard a voice say to me:

Amanda, you have two options. Option one, you stay here. Option two, you go back. And if you go back just know what you are agreeing to. Over the course of the next two years, you will go through some of the most tragic, intense, and painful experiences that a human being will ever face in a lifetime. You will be raped. You will be homeless. You will do and sell drugs. You will be in an abusive relationship. You will completely lose all of your identity. You'll be in a wheelchair. You'll gain 30 lbs. You'll begin using a walker. You'll be in the hospital for two months. You'll live in a hospital bed inside your mom's living room. You'll be $80,000 in debt. You will be on one of the deepest depressions that a human could ever feel. Do you agree? Do you consent to this contract? Do you want to sign and go back to the Earth and play out this reality? Yes or no?

The answer within my heart came up immediately. I knew it was a yes with every cell in my body and so I said with 100% clarity. Yes, I agree. In that moment, my spirit shot back into my physical body as I was lying on the operating table and the nurses began to wake me from the nine hours of anesthesia I was under.

●　●　●

First, let me take you back to where this all began.

July 24, 2010 was a sunny and beautiful summer day in Pullman, Washington. I woke up in the morning to do what I always did. Go to the gym and work with my personal training clients. It was such a beautiful morning. I loved the opportunity to make a difference in people's lives through the transformation of fitness. As the morning went on, I realized that this day was our team building activity day and all of my team was going to be meeting on the Snake River to have a celebration. The celebration was meant to include fun and play, margaritas, and wave runners.

We drove the hour long drive from Pullman and arrived in Lewiston, Idaho. I was so excited to spend time on the water. The water was one of my greatest loves in this lifetime. I had been riding wave runners since I was thirteen years old. And when I say that I'm a bit wild, I was *definitely* a bit wild and at the age of twenty-one I was also invincible. The afternoon wore on and I lay on the towel with my bubble gum pink bikini, enjoying margaritas. We would, from time to time, hop in the water and take a spin on the wave runners, and at the final ride of the night, around 7pm as the sun was setting, I was asked to take one final ride and to bring a passenger with me. One of the other trainers' husbands, Joe, saw me earlier in the day playing on the wave runners and said, "You seriously know how to ride that thing and I want to ride with you." So, I said, "Yes." We hopped on the wave runner and I began to accelerate to speeds of around thirty-five miles per hour, taking aggressive turns to the left and whipping out on the back end. Joe would fly off the seat and fly into the water. We would both laugh and we'd get back on and do it again. After doing it a second time, Joe began to take notice that he was the one flying off and I wasn't. We hopped back on the wave runner and he scooted close to me and held onto my life jacket. He held on to me so tightly, I turned my head and said, "You know that means if you fly off, I'm flying off with you." We both chuckled and let out a roaring laugh as the sun was shining down and glistening on our skin.

Just as the sun was setting, I accelerated one final time and as I turned the handlebars to the left, the difficult force of our weight sent both of our bodies off the edge of the wave runner. There was a problem. My knee got caught on the edge of the seat and as my knee tore with excruciating force, I flew across the water skipping like a big giant rock. I immediately knew that something was terribly wrong. I screamed with all of my might, "I broke my leg! I broke my leg!"

As I laid there in those dark, cool waters, I began to see my life flash before my eyes. I started seeing hobbies I enjoyed and the work I did. I started seeing myself in college walking on the campus. I started seeing myself with my family. It was this immediate review of all of the things in my life that made me who I am, or at least who I thought I was. I saw all of who I saw myself to be. The identity that I had built so profoundly around myself was that of the personal trainer, the group fitness instructor, the bodybuilder, and the fitness enthusiast. My whole identity was built around my physical body and how my physical body looked. When I woke up every morning, I focused on having a six pack of abs. I was neurotic about what I put in my body for food. I counted every calorie, protein, fat, and carb to make sure that my physical body would match the identity that I had created in my mind of what I believed was necessary in order to be loved and valued in this world.

In that moment, lying in the river was the first fracture of that identity. The 'Life Review' I was experiencing began to show me all these images of my attachment to this physical body. I quickly came to and began to direct Joe to support the transportation of getting me back to the shore. My first effort wasn't very useful; the pain in my leg was so incredibly excruciating that I could barely breathe.

I was beginning to go into shock. Every part of my body was shivering and it wasn't even cold out. I saw a family about one-hundred yards away on the shore and I screamed to them for help. I watched as the family began to pack up their belongings into their boat and make their way towards this floating woman in the river. The boat arrived and as I lay in the water, I said, "I broke my leg" and the dad said, "It's okay. We'll help you." The mom jumped into the water and selflessly went underneath the water to help lift my body up, while the dad put his arms underneath my armpits and pulled me onto the stern of the boat.

The sun had set and the sky was transitioning into that in-between gray state that happens before it's gone down. I felt the darkness begin to arise both in my external environment and within my own being. The transportation to the emergency room was one of the most painful rides of my life. Because every time the boat would hit just even a tiny bump on the water, it would send shockwaves of pain from my leg all the way through my head. We landed at the dock and the emergency medical team had already arrived. With my very commanding twenty-one-year-old presence, I stated very aggressively, "You will not move me off this boat until you put morphine in my arm. Because I am in so much pain that I'm unwilling to feel any more than this."

They listened. They injected my arm with an IV of morphine. I felt a slight sense of relief and felt the fog for the first time. The fog of my awareness being blocked by a drug. The medicine transported me into the emergency room. As we pulled up, the bright lights were shining. The hole through the lobby looked like the gates of heaven. And little did I know that it wouldn't be the first time I saw this image and it wouldn't be the last time that I saw the bright white lights that night. No. They would come again. As we rolled into the emergency room, I remember thinking to myself, Man, I know this place well.

As we rolled into the emergency room, I remember thinking to myself, Man, I know this place well.

This happened to be my twenty-first trip to the emergency room in the past eighteen years. To say I was accident prone is an understatement. My mom used to tell me that she thought I should live in a plastic bubble. The memories began to flood back of all the times that I was taken to the emergency room for stitches and for broken bones.

The doctor came in to see me and immediately said, "Well, it looks like you dislocated your patella."

"Okay, so what does that mean, doctor?" I said back to him.

"Well, what it means is we're going to pop your knee back into place and then once your knee is back into place, then we'll probably discharge you and send you home from the hospital in about three to four hours."

"Alright, that sounds great," I said.

Shortly thereafter, he came in and placed one hand on either side of my kneecap and aggressively moved it back into place. I heard a loud popping sound and the amount of pain that I felt in my body was more excruciating than the accident itself.

I said to the doctor immediately, "Oh my God! That hurts so bad. It's actually worse!"

He said, "Okay, just lie here for a few minutes and I'll come back and check on you and see how you're doing."

When he came back into my room, maybe about fifteen to thirty minutes later, I said, "Doctor, whatever you did, did not make the pain better. It actually made it worse. I need to tell you something. There is something seriously wrong with my legs!"

"I understand. Let's take the next step and do a CT scan." The nurses rolled me from the cold, white emergency room. The stretcher was rolled into the operating imaging room. I could hear the sound of the imaging machine and it felt like fingernails on a chalkboard. The paramedics lifted me up and placed me onto the imaging table. They put my body through the scanner and began to hear this loud shaky noise as the images were taken. The fear and uncertainty I was feeling in my body at that moment were unlike anything I had ever felt in my entire life. I knew that something was wrong no more than five minutes after the scan was complete. The emergency room doctor showed up in my room and said, "Amanda, I have some bad news for you. You dislocated your patella and you also tore all four ligaments in your knee. You severed the main artery in your lower leg. So, if we don't get you into surgery within the next hour, you will most likely lose your leg. Your helicopter is on its way. We're going to transport you to the closest vascular hospital. When you land, they're going to do an emergency vascular surgery to repair your artery so that you don't lose your leg."

Fear took over my body in such a way that I was paralyzed. I didn't have any words to say. I didn't think I was even thinking any thoughts until finally I said, "Can someone please go with me?" I didn't want to be alone. I was scared. The doctor said, "Unfortunately, there's no there's no room in the helicopter except for you and the pilots. You'll be okay. They'll take care of you."

They began to prepare for the transition to the helicopter pad and I could see the propellers turning, creating so much force of air in the space and I knew at that moment that my life was about to significantly change.

It was forty-five minutes of the deepest, darkest battle I had ever faced, yet there were many more to come. The thoughts that began to circle in my head were things like, *What if I lose my leg? Will I ever be able to walk again? Am I going to have a fake leg? Who's gonna want to be with me if I have a fake leg? Am I going to gain weight? What's going to happen to my business? Am I ever going to be able to train clients again?*

All of the stories began to cycle, which created more and more of the energy of fear and more and more of the energy of anxiety and worry. As the helicopter landed on the tarmac in Spokane, Washington, Dr. Robertson was there waiting for my arrival as they rolled me from the stretcher into the hospital directly towards the operating room.

He said to me, "Amanda, I have to tell you everything that could transpire, because there are many outcomes possible. Number one: no guarantees you're going to have your leg when you wake up in the morning. If you still have your leg, there are no guarantees you're ever going to be able to walk or run ever again. Do you understand?"

"Yes. I understand."

"I have to also tell you this: the surgery that I am about to do on you is called a FEM pop procraft. I'm going to cut open the inner part of your leg and the incision will be about fifteen inches long. I'm going to take two inches of your femoral artery and I'm going to attach it to your popliteal artery. I've only done this surgery successfully one time. The surgery will take me approximately nine hours. That is twice as long as it would take me to do open heart surgery on you. So the risk is extremely high. I need you to know that I will do my best. Now, we need to put you under anesthesia."

The nurse placed a cold plastic face covering over my mouth and nose. "Take a few deep breaths. And when I say go you're going to count backwards from ten.

At the same time I'm going to be injecting anesthesia directly into your arms as well as having you breathe through this inhaler. Count backwards from ten. Nine, eight…"

By the time I made it to seven I was gone. My consciousness was no longer in my body. *Where did it go?* My spirit had detached from my physical form, and it had gone back to the place where all spirits come from, the white light. The light of divinity. My connection to source and my agreement to return to this planet was anchored into my spirit in this moment. I woke up in the morning in the ICU. The nurse gently shaking my shoulder. "Amanda. Amanda. Amanda, wake up. Amanda, wake up. Amanda wake up!!"

Groggily, I opened my eyes just barely. I was on so many drugs. *What is happening?* "Amanda, do you know where you are?"

"No."

"Do you know what's happening?"

"No." I wasn't just in a state of confusion, I was in a state of utter disbelief. I was shocked that my spirit was now back in this physical body. I was so numb that I couldn't fully feel what had actually happened. My mom had arrived on an overnight flight and was standing at the foot of my bed. As I opened my eyes, she looked like an actual angel. The bright, white hospital lights and the cold hospital room glowing down on her head, like a halo.

"Hi sweetie," she said.

"Hi mom."

"You're doing a really good job."

I can only imagine what was running through her mind as she observed me, lying semi-lifeless in this hospital. Four days and four nights I was in the ICU as the doctor treated my body with medicine, painkillers, antibiotics, and antivirals. I looked down at my leg and I said to my mom, who was gazing at me with deep concern, "At least I still have my leg."

"That's right."

It took me about a week before I really began to gain any sort of understanding of what had actually happened as the drugs slightly started to lift from my system. I was lying in the dark room and in the wee hours of the morning, my mom lay in the chair by my bed. I could tell that she was half asleep and half awake with her awareness focused on me. And so I whispered, "Hey, Mom."

"Yes," she said.

"I have something to tell you."

"What's that honey?" The energy in the room was palpable.

"I will fucking walk again!"

The next two months were a constant struggle with pain, followed by more pain. The doctor injected me with massive amounts of painkillers, and sleeping pills were the only thing that would give me any relief. It was then that I learned that if I didn't want to feel pain, I just needed to sleep. Visitors came and went and my room was filled with an overflowing abundance of flowers, but I couldn't see the beauty because it was clouded. With my view of the darkness, depression had taken over my body like a virus infecting my entire being. Fear was clinging on to me with all its might. Surgery followed surgery, and five surgeries later, after two months in the hospital, I knew that my life would consist of bedrest accompanied by a bedpan and catheter, at least for now.

Finally, I began the journey to the commitment that I made weeks before and as the nurse began to slowly help me sit up, she said, "Today we're going to begin the process to help you learn how to walk again."

On my very first try I was able to stand up and put my leg down for ten seconds. 1001, 1002, 1003, 1004, 1005, 1006, 1007, 1008, 1009, 1010, and then I would have to lie back down and elevate my legs so quickly as the blood rushed back into my body. The pain was so excruciating I realized that was the maximum that I could do at that moment. The process was slow and arduous. It felt like no progress was being made. So much of my perspective was shattered by the heaviness of the drugs and the darkness of the fear. There was bitterness, anger, rage, guilt, and shame. *How could I have done this to myself? How could I have ruined my entire life?*

When I was discharged from the hospital at the two month mark, I started to have a little bit more hope for the future. Although bleak, it would come and go in the midst of the waves of depression and hopelessness. I, a helpless victim, would think: *Why me? Why this? Why my leg? Why my body? Why the thing that is everything to me?* Days, then months, moved slowly like molasses. Physical therapy sessions day after day. Then, physical therapy sessions two times a day, five days a week. For six months, that was my entire life.

I was watching my senior year of college unfold on Facebook from the hospital bed in my mom's living room, as I popped OxyContin and Percocet all day long just to manage being in this body. The addiction to the painkillers was so high that I couldn't go hours without receiving medication. Otherwise, I would start to have withdrawals. Until one day, I said to my mom, "Enough is enough! I will not become my brother. I will not have a heroin addiction. I'm done. I am fucking done. I am not taking another pill. You can't make me, no one can make me and I'm done."

I drew a line in the sand that day to make sure that the heaviness of the numbing of my life was gone. It was the most challenging four days of my life as my body detoxed from the massive amount of opiates that the doctor had been pumping into my twenty-one year-old system for the previous six months. I sweated through the sheets four nights in a row while my mom took care of me, comforting me as I shivered and as I sweated profusely from every pore in my body; letting go, letting go, letting go.

● ● ●

I wish I could say that everything got better from that point on. But, I remembered that wasn't the agreement that I signed. I did not sign an agreement that read: "You're going to have an accident and then you're going to get better." That's not what I signed. I signed an agreement that said you're gonna have an accident and now you're going to begin two years of darkness. My conscious awareness didn't have that understanding.

Following the surgeries and recovery, I now had to face another enemy. As the darkness began to take over my life; the sex, drugs, alcohol, abuse and the rape, it began to manifest in my reality like a demon holding on to my physical body. So much darkness. So much pain. So much fear. So much agony. Until finally, one day, I made a decision that enough was enough. I drew another line in the sand and I stated a claim for my life. I said, *My life will not continue down this path. If I stay in the city, I'm going to end up dead or in prison.* The selling of the drugs had taken over my life. The abuse from my partner had beaten me down. My self worth and self value and identity had completely crumbled. I did not know who I was anymore, months had turned into a year and I now felt more lost than ever before. But, there was a spark still within me. A spark in my spirit that came through in that moment of clarity said, *You do not deserve this. You do not deserve this life. You do not deserve darkness. You do not deserve it. You are worthy. You are loved. You are lovable. You are beautiful. You are brilliant. You are special.* The voice of God speaking directly to me, reminding me of who I really was. Those words of encouragement. Those words of light going into my reality began to change everything for me. They allowed me the courage to begin to step forward to pack up my car and move to different cities, and to take courageous steps towards the future reality that I wanted to create.

Even though it was hard, and even though it meant leaving my family and my friends and everything that I knew to begin again, I knew with every part of me that it was the most important step I could ever take. Thank God that when I arrived in Arizona, I began working for a company and found a mentor who said to me, "Amanda, you are the most resilient person I have ever met in my entire life. And if you start working on yourself every day, what you will accomplish in this lifetime will be unlike anything I've ever seen. You have such a capacity for leadership." I didn't fully believe him, but he believed in me just enough so that it gave me a little hope to begin my journey of transformation; the journey of healing that had been prophesied about when I accessed the light. The agreement said, *Remember Amanda, two years of the most pain any human could ever feel followed by ten years of healing, but once that ten years of healing is complete, your life will be blessed.* So the journey began.

They say the journey of 10,000 miles begins with the first step. This is true. The journey of 10,000 miles begins underneath your feet; step by step, day by day, moment by moment, person by person. My life began to change. It began to transform, to unfold, to expand, to blossom. One of my greatest opportunities was beginning to craft a new identity. One that was honoring the totality of my being, not just my physical form. One that understood the truth of who I really am. The remembrance of my infinite, spiritual nature that this body is just a vessel in this lifetime for this soul's experience, but that I will continue to live on in the spirit forever and ever in eternity.

Although the accident, and the pain and the suffering that came because of it, at the time felt like one of my life's greatest tragedies, I now know that that experience was one of life's greatest gifts. At the age of twenty-one, and in the integration through the years beyond, I learned that I am light. I learned that I am infinite. I learned that no matter what anyone else says, I know who I am. It wasn't an easy path. It hasn't been an easy journey, but it's been so worth it. The transformation that I've been able to take myself through, and to be supported by so many incredible people in my life, now allows me a level of compassion that I never had before. A love for the world that I never knew was possible before the accident. I feel so deeply the pain of those that are around me. I feel so deeply the pain of the world. The sadness, the grief, the anger, the rage. I feel it all. I also have more compassion for the homeless; I know what it's like to be in a wheelchair and I know what it's like to be addicted to drugs. I know what it's like to be raped and I know what it's like to be in abusive relationships. I also know what it's like to build a massive company. I know what it's like to fly on a private jet and I know what it's like to travel all around the world and lie on some of the world's most beautiful beaches. I know what it's like to love with my whole heart and what a gift that is. What a gift to have that level of knowing in this lifetime.

What a gift to have such a high level of awareness that I am not my body. I have a body, but I am not my body. I also have fingernails, but I am not fingernails. I am infinite light and so are you.

If we as humans begin to look at life's greatest obstacles as life's greatest gifts, the world would begin to transform. It wouldn't allow the human mind to get stuck in the trap of fear, anger, guilt, and shame, but to elevate and rise above and to see life for the beauty that it is. To see each other through eyes of compassion. To live with reckless abandon. To live life fully. To love each other fully and be committed to having the influence and the transformation that we are here to make on this planet and in this lifetime, actually occur.

If we as humans begin to look at life's greatest obstacles as life's greatest gifts, the world would begin to transform.

● ● ●

I am the light of divinity.
My essence is infinity.
Infinitely kind and beautiful is she.
The best thing is she knows who she be.
She knows who she be and who she is becoming.
Always patient, never running, never rushing,
always listening and being guided by intuition.

Amanda Goolsby

Amanda Goolsby is the founder of The Goolsby Group, a leadership and business coach, and international speaker. Amanda gained real life rapid business scaling experience through supporting the development and launch of over 50 locations of the Orangetheory Fitness Brand globally.

She has spent a decade and hundreds of thousands of dollars in deeply studying leadership, personal transformation, high-performance, meditation, and wellness. For the last eight years she has owned her own coaching & consulting business, supporting hundreds of entrepreneurs to launch and scale their businesses all over the world.

Although currently based in Austin, Texas, you can find Amanda optimizing her health wherever she is in the world. She is a luxury spa connoisseur and often can be found submerging herself in a cold plunge or freezing cold body of water!

CONNECT WITH AMANDA

 @amandagoolsbywellness 🏠 ExquisiteLeadershipExperience.com

CHAPTER 5

Go Within to Heal, the Power is Inside

By Laura Lee Lotto

August 2015

Sitting on my cold cement front porch, cupping my face in my hands, bent over my black yoga pants in complete surrender, I rocked back and forth making sounds that were incoherent and animal-like, my mind desperately grasping at any sense of reality. Trying to come back from… where? What did I say? Who was that person? Feeling scared, angry, and mostly, ashamed, the tears started to spill over my eyes, not from sadness yet, no…this was from rage. A visceral experience trapped inside me, vibrating frantically, threatening to explode like a screaming tea kettle at its boil, I opened my mouth and allowed the intense fiery emotions that were eating me alive inside to break free and explode like a bomb through my vocal chords, grateful we lived in the country with few neighbors to hear me roar.

The day had started out like most days. Phillip was up early to milk the two big, white Saanen goats we had, that always reminded me of marshmallows; sweet and round! We loved fresh goat milk and were really enjoying it, but the demand of milking animals day in and day out was taking its toll on us both. He usually fed the chickens and picked the eggs too, and let them all out to forage in the long grass for the day, to excitedly find their grubs and bugs. I was in bed, attempting to get a few more precious minutes of sleep while nursing Miss Gwenivere who had just turned two a few weeks earlier. She was dozing in and out of consciousness in her three-sided crib I made at woodshop class when I was pregnant with her brother six years earlier. I liked having the crib attached to our bed and that the kids were always near me, but still had their own space.

Three-year-old Gertie was zonked out in the room she shared with her brother right next to ours. I could hear Elliott was awake by the infamous sound of a little kid's hand rummaging through a Lego box looking for that very specific piece. How Gertie could sleep through that, I had no idea, but she was one of those amazing people who could sleep through fighter jets overhead. That incessant 'searching through pieces' sound seemed amplified in my head like I was in an echo chamber as I woke up to it day after day. I couldn't do anything to make him stop and was forced to listen to all of the tiny colored bricks being pushed up against the hard plastic blue bin. I surrendered to the fact that I would not get any more sleep that day, while I nursed and stared at the god-awful ugly, dark-brown-paneled walls of our not-yet-remodeled bedroom. I was neither able to verbally ask Elliott to stop for fear of waking the potentially crabby toddler, nor could I get out of bed physically yet, being held down by her vigorous nursing. It had been a long night and I had been up at least four times, so I was keenly aware that moods and energies, particularly mine, were precarious already. So there I lay, able to do nothing but tune into the irritating sound grinding into my nerves, and it was only 7:15am. Goodie. Breathe Laura, breathe.

Eventually, I was able to remove myself from the nursing hostage situation of toddler #2 to toss my large, red Laura-Ashley robe over my hairy legs, pink and white striped undies and well-worn 'Body by Ben & Jerry's' t-shirt I owned for 15 years that used to be a sage-type color. I had to move slowly to adjust and allow my aching back and stiff joints to remember their job was to move, as I quietly passed the room of Planet Lego and passed-out toddler #1, down the hall to the stove where the tea kettle awaited my arrival. After filling it and cranking the knob to high, I stared blankly at the black, glass-topped stove, vaguely wondering how much I would actually get done that day, and how much I *had* to get done that day. I could feel the fatigue from the night-time wakings pulling at me. I was always so tired and in so much pain those last few years.

Too bad…The garden was overflowing with produce, and we had farm shares to prepare and get ready for the next day so the kids and I had harvesting to do while Phillip was at work. That meant I needed to get ready for a good long while outside, which meant I had to bring the wagon with toys and snacks to keep the girls occupied while I attempted to focus the imaginative five-year-old to help me pick as much as we could, as fast as we could. Not that his Taurus Sun, Moon, and Mercury ever allowed him to move at any pace but his own steady, somewhat mind-numbing speed, but I was still at a point in life where I was attempting to push all of his Earth with all of my Air—my words. It didn't work. I would also need to set up our little blue kids tent for them for shade as it was going to be a hot day, for a Wisconsin August anyway. We would be hauling in a ton of produce too so I would need to have the wheel barrow up there as well. Sigh…I loved harvest time, but it got super overwhelming super fast, much like mothering.

My mind had disappeared down the rabbit hole of the 'invisible to-do list' that parents run all day long, the one that never ends, and has continuous additions to it, but the sharp, high-pitched bark down the hall suddenly pulled me out of my planning and prepping trance, telling me I needed to let the dogs out to pee soon, but they would have to wait as I had to take care of my own needs first. While the water heated, I dashed from the squishy blue anti-fatigue-rug I was standing on, around the kitchen corner, to the one tiny bathroom we all shared in our 1,100 sq. ft. home. I did what I could to spruce it up, but it was in desperate need of a renovation, too, with its light green paint over the old brown panels and cold, broken tile floor. The bathroom was on the list of things to fix, like everything else that cost large sums of money, waiting for us to figure out our finances.

I flushed the toilet and yanked my undies up when I heard the quick sharp bark again coming from the mud room. Someone needed to go outside quickly, but I decided to make them wait an extra forty seconds, as I grabbed the purple toothbrush and attempted to do a small bit of daily self-care. It was still weird brushing my teeth when I was missing so many and had to use a partial denture. It had been over a year since losing eight of my molars at only 31 years old, not all at once, but within a three-month span of time. My frustration and embarrassment was something I dealt with daily, but on this particular day, I didn't have much energy to put into the teeth subject except to give them a quick scrub.

I think it was Sarah who had been barking but sometimes it was hard to identify. Our four dogs, Mabel, Dahlia, Sarah and Augen, were really good, but they were still four dogs, which was a lot. It didn't used to feel like 'a lot' when I was in my professional dog-training days, doing animal rescue work, and was still waiting for the children to manifest into physical form, but now that there were three kids here, and all still very physically demanding, the dogs were yet another daily chore on that damn to-do list I couldn't ever seem to make smaller. Deep breath Laura… One more, it's free.

Phillip and I were pouring ourselves into doing a weekly farmer's market and farm shares in our small fishing town of 2,000 people. We had been planting more and more fruit trees, berry bushes, tending large plots of vegetable gardens, milking goats and raising meat birds, all with the hope of sustaining ourselves with food and eventually, financially. I was desperate to bring in income any way I could. Even though Phillip was working full time, we had been struggling financially, and adding Gwenivere to the team two years earlier made it really difficult for me to work outside the home, or really work on much of anything. Besides the kids and what I could do on the farm, I was also attempting to grow a small side business and was being trained in aromatherapy and other natural modalities.

In what seemed like no time at all, the kids were everywhere and nowhere all at once. Attempting to feed us all and clean up while simultaneously trying to get them ready to go out to the garden was making my brain feel like it was trapped inside a pinball machine. We needed to get out there before it got too hot. No cooperation was happening and my patience was thinning.

It was building…It was all building too much, too fast! Any coping skills I had (which were few) were flying out the door rapidly as my blood pressure shifted, my Cortisol skyrocketed, and my body headed off on the Fight, Flight, or Freeze train. I tried so hard to keep it in, put the lid on, stay calm, but every little sound, every little cry, demand, need…it all built up, adding to the stress pile inside my mind making the cracks widen. The needs of this child, the noises of that one. The fighting from those two, the hunger of this one who doesn't want the food I made. The pressure inside me was building up intensely, yet I was determined to keep that lid on tight! I *had to*. Breathe, Laura….Breathe, damnit!

"Brush your teeth Please! Gertie! Put pants on! Let's get to the garden PLEASE! Come! On! Let's go!" I raised my voice a little more, and there was an edge now, yet they did not listen.

I had to strain the goat milk and get that put away in the fridge before we went out. It was my job to do that part after Phillip did the milking. "Elliott! Clean up the milk on the floor please." I had to ask my oldest as I stopped Toddler #2 from nose diving into the corner of the cabinet.

"No! Please don't lick the cat!" I yelled at the three-year-old as I turned around… Someone in my mind laughing (somewhat insanely at this point) at the things I didn't think I would ever need to say. My temper rising… my patience bucket was empty.

"We don't feed the dogs our breakfast Honey!"… Ding!… Ping! The notifications of the computer, social media, the outside world, REAL People, were calling to me. My brain went in that direction, instantly wanting to escape the demands of parenting, and check out into the land of "likes" and other lost mamas where we could bitch about what we were stuck in…

"Where is a towel? Can someone bring me one? Elliott!!!" I yelled as I nearly slipped on the goat milk running across the tile. Cleaning up the mess I could feel the shifting energy inside of me. I knew something was coming. I didn't know when or what would trigger it, but I knew my buzzer was about to go off.

The weight of it all and the heavy responsibilities along with the chronic pain amplified the chaos. Having the planet Uranus in your birth chart in the Sixth House of day to day work, routine and health, leads to sudden and unexpected changes and disruption in health and daily life. Being aware of it doesn't change the fact that it happens, nor does it give you an answer on how to deal with it. When all of the intensity and chaos and change swirls inside the pressure cooker, well, it eventually gets too much and it blows. I blew up.

Wounded, broken, inadequate…when things around me felt so disintegrated that I suffered like I was actually splitting apart and in doing so, I was losing my mind. How can these phenomenal, beautiful children…something I longed for so deeply for so long, be the exact thing causing this moment?

I felt these feelings oh so many years earlier when I was yearning for them to come. How are these feelings reoccurring so many years later because of the children? Isn't that just the thing of it though? It's the same coin, just viewed from different sides. The polarization of the poles, equal parts attractive as they are repelling. This is who I am and something I've had to work hard to embrace over the years. This… this intensity, this force, the harsh words, and this energy that comes from me when I am out of balance, and not just 'sort of' out of balance. No, these episodes don't happen unless I'm *REALLY* out of balance and have not taken care of myself.

It's not like I enjoy kicking myself out of my own home so I don't cause any more damage with my sharp tongue than what's already been done. This time, I had all three children crying with the intense screaming frustration that came out of me. The last straw being the cat food tipped upside down all over the floor where I just cleaned up the milk. My sweet, sensitive youngest child, Gwenivere, was crying the hardest as she is so, so affected by my intensity with her 55% water planets in her birth chart, and she doesn't handle these intense outbursts from me well at all.

Who can blame her? How is a toddler supposed to handle her mama having a tantrum? I was freaking out about dirty dishes, spilled milk and cat food, toys that never get picked up and an endless to-do list running through my mind. I looked like a toddler who missed my nap as I was yelling and having my own breakdown party, grabbing and throwing whatever random item was laying in front of me and didn't belong there. I was yelling so loud at no one, and everyone, and angry at myself for losing my shit again! Why can't I keep it together? Why must I fall down the "screaming rabbit hole"? It's just all so much and my head felt out of my control! I had to force myself to go outside, out of sheer desperation to get myself to STOP! Stop being mean and blaming kids for being kids! So much blame! Where did it come from?

In these moments, I couldn't think and my brain felt like there were two escaped convicts running rampant who are insistent on doing as much damage in the shortest amount of time as possible. These two psychopathic women usually lived in a tan padded room with bad lighting, kept safely secured with their straight jackets on, in the back right side of my brain. They were always kept under tight lock and key with twenty-four-hour surveillance. At that point in my life, they were making frequent escape attempts and were causing some serious issues.

It felt like my mouth WAS being controlled by someone else. The shame I felt when I looked into my children's eyes. A blank, non-expression, reflected back at me, meaning they had shut down entirely, and retreated to their internal 'safe spaces' far away from me. Looking into those expressionless eyes, I felt the pang of a sword enter my heart when realization hit, and I recognized they had run away from ME, their safety, to find their own shelter. I felt the confusion that it caused inside of them, not understanding why their mother would be so harsh for seemingly no reason. Twist, the sword cut and sliced the arteries causing me to finally feel something OTHER than rage. Their scared retreat from my intense words were what brought me back to some semblance of reality so I could see, feel, and eventually make the rational decision to get the hell out of the house for a moment! Get myself together and calm down for ONE minute. But these skills aren't taught in any pregnancy classes I took. No one informed me of the true insanity that comes with parenting three small children.

In these moments of rage, because that's what it was—hormonally imbalanced rage—,I was keenly aware of the *crazy* that was flying out of me and was written all over my aura, my body, my everything. I felt like I got 'stuck' in the observer-mode and the rational person who was normally in charge couldn't get back to the "mouth panel" and gain control over what was flying out of it. I intellectually knew and understood I needed to take the "anger costume" off and sit down and cry…to just *feel*, dammit…But I was stuck in the anger, the shame, the anger, the shame…the trauma cycle of generational baggage, on top of hormonal imbalance, and a toxic, pain-filled, sleep-deprived, exhausted, mama body.

I paced the five front porch steps up and down, and the small concrete stoop at the bottom, staying in that area because in my furry I didn't grab shoes, otherwise I'd be halfway around the trails in our young spruce woods by now, walking off this intense anger energy. It was taking a huge amount of focused, mindful effort for me to calm the rage when it built like this. I know it doesn't just happen, and there are always underlying reasons that are way deeper and they are getting triggered by the chaos of my daily life, so I have to calm myself enough to figure out what my immediate needs are, but how does one find balance when out of balance?

After some time of going through situations like this, I've learned that usually I need to sit down to soften the anger, pull my Fire and Air elements down into the tiny amount of Water element I have, and finally, feel... cry...I cried a hard, ugly, intense cry, one that allowed the chaos, the generational trauma, the shame, guilt and other emotional pain to flood forward out my eyeballs. These ugly cries forced me to release as if I'm vomiting emotions out of my guts, and came out as strong sobbing, and dripping as snot out my nose and drool out my mouth. I surrendered to the power that was rage, now transformed and released in a softer, less harmful way. (Ugly cries are the worst and I avoided them like the plague, which clearly wasn't working for me as the yelling outbursts were getting bad.)

As I sat and cried, in my mind, I pulled up an image of my astrology chart; I was 64% air signs, 23% fire, a mere 13% water, and no planets were in earth signs the day I was born. The pie chart of the image made me understand that I do burn hot with very little to anchor me except a little glass of water...and it's OKAY...It's a big work in progress to accept myself, *all* of myself...Fire and Air burn, and they can also warm a space and bring people together.

I had to learn to accept my elemental gift and learn to manage it. No one taught me this, I taught myself. Breathe, Laura. I told myself, "Hang on, you can get through this. You've done it before." I focused on calming the fireball that was me and bringing it down to a warm fireplace burn

> I had to learn to accept my elemental gift and learn to manage it.

and not the exploding Roman Candle firework that had previously exited the house, going off at any little thing.

It was only a few minutes of that profound crying and in those moments of purging, I found some of the fog that flooded my mind and heart had lifted a bit and wasn't as dense as it was before the cry. It felt like the storm was moving on and I could take control of the wheel again. There was still a lot to do to make sure we could sail again, but the eye of the hurricane had passed, for the most part.

Next, I needed to access the fix-it tools I had been acquiring over the years and stashed in my self-care toolbelt. I needed to re-establish some semblance of harmony within me. I didn't have many in the toolbelt yet, but I was learning from these experiences that before anything else, I needed to get my hormones balanced. I have had a long and arduous journey learning to understand my hormones, and when I didn't get the message, then freakouts like this day's episode would happen.

Slowly removing my head from the cold, metal railing I had leaned against, I wiped the snot and tears from my face with the cuff of my dirty-gray garden hoodie and stood up. I deliberately walked into the house, not wanting to look at, or talk to, the kids yet as I still couldn't trust myself. I was doing better, but I knew I could flare easily, like a secondary fire can start if all the embers aren't put out.

I headed straight to the relief I so desperately needed, and thankfully, that black metal shelf with the trees and birds on it that held my oils was only a few steps from the front door. It took just a moment for me to find my small, clear bottle of Progessence Plus serum. I dropped several drops (extra this day as it was clearly a tough one) onto my forearms and rubbed them together. Within moments, it would flood my blood stream with the supporting substances my body needed to help bring balance to my adrenals and mind. High cortisol and low progesterone is an under-diagnosed health problem in women and can cause mental health episodes as well as brain fog and overwhelming mood swings. I only would behave in this intense way, and those two crazy women would only get out of their padded room, when my progesterone levels had really tanked.

As I sat down on the floor and stared at the clock, I knew relief was on its way. I was doing it, doing the work. One step at a time. Breathe Laura, breathe. The panic and fear of a resurgence of anger was still high. I closed my eyes again and had an urge to run and call Phillip...my safety, my anchor. "I NEED to call Phillip!" someone shouted loudly in my head. "He can calm this! He can save us!" I heard, almost as a chant, several times over from somewhere deep inside. The feeling of desperation was still coursing through me. There has always been this deep urge inside me for someone to help me, do it with me, anchor me, thanks to my three planets in Libra... sign of relationships, balance, peace, justice and harmony. But really, there is no one except me who ever truly rescued me. My lesson with Saturn in Libra and located in the Fifth House of children, fun and play, was going to eventually teach me that I needed to find peace and balance inside of myself, not from an outside source.

This was a lesson I would have ample opportunity to learn throughout the small moments of the day, the really hard moments, when all I could do is take deep breaths, and rescue myself from one minute to the next. From one pain surge to the next moment when the pain let go enough for me to move. From one scarcity moment to the next gratitude moment. It's always me, going inside, calming my own storm, my own chaos, and my own fears. I was the one having to dig deep and pull out the deep shit I didn't know I had in me to stabilize, heal, and love myself enough to make whatever changes that needed to be made.

I forced myself to breathe slowly with my hands cupped over my face taking in the aroma part of aromatherapy. I closed my eyes and remained seated and breathed, even though my mind still raced. I had managed to capture the crazy ladies and haul them back to their cells, but there were still people rioting in the streets, needs still unmet, and general turmoil going on inside.

Outside of me my attention was grabbed by the youngest toddler who was still lightly crying. Her storm was passing as well and I instinctively knew I needed to tend to her, but I couldn't just yet. I wasn't quite stable myself. Her eyes, so sad, so lost, dripped tears and her fist rubbed snot all over her chubby face and then into her shirt.

It's almost incomprehensible and nearly impossible to explain the shame I felt when I spoke in a way that hurt the kids. If anyone else ever talked to me the way I let go sometimes, I would kill that person dead on the spot with my third-eye laser beam. For some reason though, I allowed these powerful, deep hurts, angers, and nasty words to flow from my mouth like it was controlled by another being!

Gertie cautiously came around the corner of the stud-walled pantry we had not finished yet, unicorn stuffy tightly squeezed between her arm and body, wary and also visibly upset, but she was not actively crying anymore.

Closing my eyes again and doing nothing but focusing on my breath, I could feel the fog lifting from my brain. I glanced at the clock again... a mere eight minutes, and a sense of calmness returned like the sun breaking through the clouds after the departed storm. My amazement at the power of plants and natural healing was not able to be fully acknowledged while I dealt with the immediate needs of the moment.

As my mind was finally able to move on to the 'what's the next tool in my self-care toolbelt?' question, my oldest, Elliott, already knew what I needed, and even at the tender age of five, was keenly aware that food helped bad moods. He handed me a blue plastic toddler plate loaded with crackers, cut up apple slices, and a big ole pile of peanut butter.

Frozen in a totally new sensation and experiencing a huge emotional shift, I turned to mush inside and melted like butter on a hot stove…I smiled through my freshly formed tears, feeling both the pang of guilt for what I had said, and the tantrum I had, and feeling extreme love and gratitude at their ability to forgive. Elliott and I had been through a lot together and he wasn't as easily affected by my intense mood shifts as the girls were, and I was immensely grateful for his groundedness and for him.

I always need *food* in these mood-shifting, mental-health-crashing, chaotic hormone situations. (*insert eyeroll*…Ugh!) My mental instability is tied to food and hormonal shifts like weeding is tied to gardening, and the lack of food caused more hormonal shifts and only exacerbated the problem, which also flared my inflammation and chronic health struggles. Yippy! This was all explainable, of course, with my cortisol levels and other hormone cycles that take place, but I was still trying to piece the puzzle together and didn't know this all yet. I was lost in dealing with the emotional baggage of 'shame' that comes along with not being able to manage the daily task of feeding myself to keep my own shit together!

Food was a big issue for me, and it's not that there wasn't any, it's just that I didn't actually like to eat much (being in chronic fight/flight/flee does that) and it felt like a never ending chore. With the silent mental to-do list always running, it was a big struggle to remember, or to prioritize eating. With three small children, my self care was non-existent, and eating was part of that 'self-care.' There was just so much I had to do… And eating wasn't high on that list for me…other than for the purpose of living!

This particular day, my blood sugar had crashed because it was already 1pm and I had exactly half of a banana and two cups of earl gray tea. It was a major contributing factor to that day's meltdown and this was a theme I was seeing when I looked at the other mental health crashes that seemed to be on repeat during this time in my life. I didn't think I could do it all and I felt really desperate in my heart for help with the overwhelming responsibilities of the incredible life I had longed for, manifested, and created. I kept looking to other people for help rescuing me from me. I wanted community! I wanted to create my village! My desperation to 'do it all' and 'all at once' was leading to adrenal fatigue, and pulling me apart, I just didn't know how badly. I so deeply wanted to make our farm bring in income, and be something we could do to support ourselves.

My mind drifted as I slowly made myself eat the plate of food presented to me. E had taken it upon himself to make snack plates for him and his sisters and was making sound effects to the imagination game in his head as he worked. To reach better he was standing on the "Little Lotto Stool" I had recently made and painted purple and teal.

Chewing slowly and mindfully, I was pondering the family of six from New Mexico that came eleven months earlier to live with us and build a like-minded community with us, and in my mind, to *save me*, whatever that looked like. Nevermind I had never met them in real life before inviting them to live with us. Nevermind we had no place for them to actually live besides the living room of our two bedroom home, which was fully occupied with our own three kids, four dogs, cats, Phillip and me. My ridiculously optimistic self was so foolish thinking that I could make it work to have six additional people come and live with us and somehow that would solve my problems! What a crazy airhead I was sometimes! After three weeks of that shit-show experiment, the family packed up and headed back to the south and we got back to digging our own asses out of our own problems...for a little while anyway.

Taking a swipe of peanut butter off the plate with my finger, my mind jumped to our financial stress that was a constant nagging irritation in the background of our life that we both struggled to deal with. My flighty, ungrounded self wasn't one to stay consistent and focus on budgeting or accounting, and while, yes, Pip did manage the bills and budget, it was usually just barely, and with not much of a system in place. There was the usual playing of financial games like waiting to pay one bill to make sure another one that will charge a fee gets paid first. It had been like this most of our adult life, some years better than others, but in general, we had chronically been financially struggling.

We had also been paying cash out of pocket for the specialized testing Gertie, our fiery three year old, needed a year prior, to figure out what her unique health issues were because the medical doctors we saw didn't believe us and wouldn't do the testing we needed, and insurance didn't pay for the special tests. We had to then pay for her loads of oils and herbs she needed to heal. It just seemed like one thing after another and getting above ground was a constant struggle. Physically, we carry the emotional weight of structure, finances, and basic needs in life in our low back area. My lower back had been suffering from our financial strain, and I had been seeing a chiropractor weekly for years, but it continued to slowly deteriorate, taking a lot of my mental stability with it as the pain grew over time.

I sat on the floor of my kitchen, mentally taking note of the random kids' items strewn everywhere. I looked down at the nearly empty plate in my lap with just one apple slice and two crackers left. My nose could smell something nice but couldn't place the sweet and floral aroma. Elliott smiled and said, "I put the diffuser on with Peace & Calming. I thought that would help." Both girls had patered over to me by this time, knowing my fire had subsided and I was safe to approach again and wouldn't burn them. The three of them gathered near me like baby chicks under a mama hen.

I took a deep breath, "I'm really sorry kids. Mama didn't mean to lose control. I'm still learning how to do all of this. Learning how to be me and be a Mama. It's hard!"

Gertie snuggled in closer and said in her super sweet, high pitched, chipmunk voice, "It's al-wite Mama! We yuv yooouuu!"

Then she gave me a kiss on the cheek and said exuberantly, "I get SO MAD and I hit! But I not apposed to. It hurts!"

Elliott chimed in with, "I get really mad sometimes too and want to hit something hard!"

I smiled, gave a chuckle which felt good after all of the anger and sadness, and said, "I UNDER-stand! No one taught me how to deal with my big feelings. I didn't know what to do and people made me feel bad for having big feelings. But now I know it's who I am and I'm supposed to have these big feelings. I just need to learn how to deal with them so I don't hurt others. I don't want to hurt you with my words when I'm mad. I'm really sorry."

After lots of hugs and kisses and more hugs and some giggles, I set the kids around me in a circle on the sage green rug and I grabbed another essential oil that was laying near me. I dropped a few drops onto their feet, having them rub their adorable little toes together. I then instinctively grabbed their hands and we formed a circle: me, the two year old Gwenivere to my left, her sister Gertie to my right, and Elliott across from me, holding each other's hands. I took a deep breath and they followed. I took another. I asked, "What are you thankful for today?" and allowed each of them to reply.

Elliott went first and enthusiastically said, "I'm thankful for my new Lego Ninjago set with the Cole spinjitzu spinner! And I'm thankful for food, and my home, and my Mama feeling better."

Que heart melting into a puddle, again! Ugh! These kids! How do they do this?! They are SO fucking amazing! And so fucking infuriating! Dealing with the emotional shifts is something I was never prepared for before I became a mother.

Having one child was great and I mentally did really well. His grounded earthy self was a compliment to my fire/air combo. By the time number two came, our situation had shifted. We were selling our home and would be moving to our dream property to start our farm. A lot of shifts came rapidly when fire-child Gert showed up. We moved to our new home when she was just four months old and I was pregnant with Gwen by the time Gertie turned one year, which was CRAZY unexpected after having fertility issues for over five years!

We were not prepared at all. I was not prepared at all for the instability that would ensue after the third child came. My stress levels skyrocketed, and my physical and mental health crashed.

So when it was my turn to say what I was thankful for, I did not hesitate when I said, "I am BEYOND thankful for sitting with you three *amazing*, kids who are SO kind, and… forgiving… and I am thankful for the self-help tools I have added to my toolbelt so I can learn to calm myself down and manage my stress and emotions better to teach you better."

After we all spoke, there was some giggling while we played our made-up 'hand squeeze game' where we 'chase' each other around the circle through energy and hand squeezing.

"Let's reset! How's that sound?" I asked after blowing my nose and wiping the flowing tears that are a mix of love and sadness, still washing away the final moments of a tough few hours.

"Yeah!" they holler in unison. "Can we watch a movie?"

My mind came fully back online, calculating what the responsibilities are for the day and how much time I had left. If they watched a show in the house, I could go out to the garden by myself, have some solitude, get the picking done, and then come back and enjoy family time with them. That sounded like an AMAZING plan and I could probably get more done without them out there!

"Yes! I do believe a movie is in order! But then when that's done with, we play a game! Ok?" Cheers all around.

An hour later, I stood up straight and stretched my back which had become sore from being bent over and gathering all of the green beans I could find. I surveyed the harvest and determined it was good enough for the delivery bags of produce the next day. As I started to clean up, I took note of how genuinely amazing my life was and how far I'd truly come.

I took that moment to acknowledge that even though a lot of the trauma wasn't mine, and is generations old, I came here to heal this baggage and let it go. I was doing the work. It was happening. One breath at a time. One cry at a time. One hug at a time. I was going within to heal. The power was inside.

Laura Lee Lotto

Laura Lee Lotto is an Intuitive and Astrological Health Coach that helps people shift their perspective on all things from health, wellness, and emotional balance, to living life to the fullest. She will light a fire under your butt! She uses her bright energy to wake people up and open their eyes. By creating an open-minded and safe space, she allows clients to unpack the deep emotional trauma, usually generations old, which has built up over time and manifested into the physical pain, illness, disease or hormonal imbalance they struggle with today.

Laura draws inspiration both from her own success story and from the multitudes of success stories shared by the clients she's served over the years. Her approach takes into account the individual's astrological map, their emotional experiences throughout life, and their spiritual bodies, all of which are typically neglected when working within the allopathic model of medicine.

Laura believes in practicing what she preaches and lives as organically as possible, staying true to her beliefs. She and her husband Phillip began dating in high school and have been together for over twenty years, traveling the world, starting a farm and, after years of fertility struggle, finally have four beautiful children. Her heart's goal is to raise the next generation of bad-ass, health rebels who will fight the corporations that seek to poison us, and change the world.

CONNECT WITH LAURA

 @lauraleelotto    lauraleelotto.com

CHAPTER 6

Mastering Love

By Mary Louise Lancaster

Facebook memories can be endearing. Or they can be brutal. Little reminders of who we used to be, showing up like the Ghost of Christmas Past bringing a dried out fruit cake that's guaranteed to leave you with heartburn for the rest of the day. One particular memory, a post I made in 2014 when I was still married, humbles me every time it shows up. I was acknowledging my flaws, declaring that I was going to be a better person for myself and for the sake of my marriage. Not only did I fall short, I missed the mark by a couple hundred miles.

Even after years of struggling to keep the relationship viable and witnessing the worst part of myself come to life in the midst of trauma and chaos, I continued to validate my self-serving decisions and chose to make excuses for anything that stroked my ego. I wasn't ready to face my own faults and found ways to rationalize my behavior and justify why I was right in what I was doing. The only thing I was learning from Life School was a PhD in Justification. My personality had shifted from heart centered to full blown narcissism and I didn't even know it.

I didn't realize it then because I couldn't see past my own pain, but I was experiencing a Dark Night of the Soul. This is a stage in personal development when someone undergoes a difficult and significant transition to a deeper perception of life and learns to find their place in it. This period can last months or it can last years. It all depends on the person experiencing this rite of passage. In true Mary form, I chose the stubborn route and drew the experience out for six long years. The lessons I took away from that time of my life are invaluable and today—as hard as it has been to regurgitate the past while writing this chapter—I'm grateful for the experiences. One cannot fully appreciate the light if they don't first experience the dark.

Waking Up

At thirty-four-years-old it seemed I had it all: a husband, two kids (a boy and a girl), a house in a desirable area outside of Austin, Texas, and a well-paying career in healthcare administration. The successful life of a female executive, fulfilling every possible role she can in order to make her mark in a masculine-dominated society. I was living out the vision I had created for myself during college when I decided to make business management my major. Already married and divorced, with a two-year-old son by the time I graduated with my Bachelor's degree, I was determined to have it all. That naive girl, twelve years prior, had no clue what the reality of work/life balance was going to look like. And she damn sure didn't envision a huge self-inflicted pitfall in her perfect dream.

On the surface it appeared as if I had achieved my goal. But inside, I was miserable. I was driving over an hour each way into the city for a job that was demanding my attention like a spoiled two-year-old brat. On-call 24/7 with unreliable direct care staff, my job dictated my every move. I couldn't even plan time away without fear of being called to problem solve a staffing or patient crisis. I was watching from afar as my kids were growing up without me, unable to attend many of their school functions and celebrate their accomplishments in real time. After years of marital counseling I continued to break my promises and betray my husband. I was living a life of dishonesty and had boarded a vessel called "Deceit and Lies" to leave my soul on the shore and pursue my ego's interests. I lost complete touch with myself and didn't even know who I was or what I wanted anymore, drowning under waves of self-destruction with no end in sight.

In order to distract myself from my misery I did other odd jobs outside of my fifty+ hour salaried job to bring me back to moments of joy. I worked as a massage therapist at a chiropractor's office on the weekends, and with a young man with autism in the evenings. I always had a knack for photography and had a nice camera so I also took jobs as a photographer anywhere I could. That's how I ended up in a bride's dressing room at a wedding in May of 2012.

I had been feeling ill the past few weeks but I was determined to keep my promise to the couple. Letting someone else down to take care of myself wasn't a concept I was familiar with at that time so I showed up, even though I had been running a fever and was so weak I could barely hold myself up. My constant cough caught the attention of one of the bride's friends, a counselor by trade, who had made her way into energy healing in addition to traditional talk therapy. She looked at me with a concerned smile and commented that I must have a blockage in my heart chakra. At that time, I wasn't fully aware of what she was talking about. I knew very little about what chakras were, but I knew I'd always been sensitive when it comes to matters of the heart, so I joked, "Well, I'm a Pisces so there's always something going on with my heart."

Throughout the afternoon we talked off and on, mostly me asking questions about what her comment meant and how she could help me. She eventually offered me her business card, and as I took it from her there was an electric spark that went through my fingertips and jolted my chest. I almost felt as if someone took my breath away. I had no idea how to explain this when it happened, but I can clearly see now that it was a wake-up call from my soul, begging me to get my shit together and align myself back into a place of love.

At the reception I rushed to get all of the necessary pictures, sitting down frequently to keep from blacking out. With several hours still on the clock, I knew I had to leave before I made a spectacle and ruined this lovely couple's wedding. I excused myself early and drove straight to a minor emergency clinic where I was diagnosed with the flu and walking pneumonia. They said I'd likely had it for a while and urged me to go home and stay in bed for the next week.

I did rest for a few days, but the anxiety of staying away from the office for too long was far worse than the idea that my body was recovering from a very serious illness. *What if someone needed me? What if the State came in for their annual inspection? What if, what if, what if.* So many unknowns and my need to control forced me out of bed way too soon and back to the office.

Two weeks after the wedding, I serendipitously came across the energy healer's number. I rarely took a lunch break, but that day something inside me told me I didn't have a choice. A few days later I was sitting in her office with no idea what to expect. The only thing I did know was that I was drowning, and I felt like God had moved through this woman and handed me a lifesaver in the form of a business card.

The Confession

Four years prior to my awakening, I was underwater for different reasons. Five years into my second marriage, my husband and I had a mortgage we couldn't afford, a two-year-old daughter, and struggled with credit card debt. The model American Family. In order to get out of debt and get a better job my husband decided to get his degree. In order to make it a quick and painless process we determined it was in our best interest to move six hours away to the small west Texas town where I had gotten my degree eight years prior. We could live on campus and have minimal expenses, he could finish in two years, then we could move back to central Texas and resume our lives. We made the decision in May, and by August we had sold just about everything we owned, including our home, and moved across the state. We both landed jobs at the university; he was the resident assistant for married housing, and I was working with a grant program for first year students. He was having a blast enjoying the college experience, even though we were both thirty. And I was enjoying the much slower pace of life in the sleepy little town of only five thousand people.

When spring break came around we both had the week off, and finally enough money to enjoy some time away, so we booked a trip to Las Vegas. This would be our first real vacation as a couple, and we were both really looking forward to it. We arranged for our daughter to stay with his parents who lived just outside of Austin, and booked our airfare to fly in and out of Austin. The six-hour drive over there was filled with chatter and anticipation of the week ahead, much different than the six-hour dive back would be.

The week started out with excitement anyone might experience on their first trip to Vegas. The moment we arrived our ears hummed as slot machines clamored in disjointed unison as someone won twenty-five cents here or a dollar there. The atmosphere was electrically charged with excitement of even the smallest of wins, and patrons continued to feed the machines their hard-earned money, dignity, and respect. We had no schedule—we were just going to wing it and see where the journey took us. The lights, the sights, the sounds...all designed to mesmerize the senses. We took it all in; shopping, dining, sightseeing, and of course gambling. We even opted to take a timeshare tour where we were presented two tickets to a Circ du Soleil show on our second-to-last night in town.

The show venue was inside the Bellagio, just off of the gambling floor. There were slot machines strategically placed outside the concert hall doors and as we waited for them to open, we sat side by side in pleather chairs, feeding pennies into the mouths of the steel beasts.

At this point my memory goes blank for a moment, as is often the case when someone suffers a traumatic incident. I can't recall the few minutes between the time we sat down until he looked at me and said: "Something happened." Immediately, my heart sank. I knew, of course, what he was talking about. I'd known since the night a few months back when he came home, later than usual, going straight to the shower before inching his way silently into bed and facing the wall. Of course I knew then, but I wasn't ready to live in that reality. I chose to make excuses for his behavior: "He was just being considerate...His friends smoke so he was washing the smell off...He didn't want to wake me...." I never brought it up, never asked him about it. But at that moment I didn't have a choice. He was forcing a shift in my alternate reality and securely strapping me in for the wildest ride of my life.

The remainder of our trip is a bit of a blur. I struggled between wanting to remain indifferent, to having a nervous breakdown in a very public place. Although, I'm not sure anyone would have recognized the difference between the meltdown of a woman whose husband just admitted an affair and a woman who just won the million-dollar slot tournament. But I kept my composure, shoving all those emotions down as far as I could manage. Pretending like it was acceptable because of a conversation we'd had pre-children about a "don't ask, don't tell" relationship, and going out of my way to make sure he knew what he would be missing out on if he ever left.

On the last full day of our trip I woke up completely covered in hives. The stress on my body was too much and my inner voice was screaming to be let out. I just wanted to get through the next two days and get home so I continued to quiet it. The tears, the rage, the revenge would come, just not that day.

The next several months I prolonged my misery and stayed on the path of denial. I continued to pretend to be okay with what happened, taking on the blame because I had agreed to an open relationship years before. I was setting both of us up for failure, though, because I wasn't acknowledging my heartbreak and he had no idea how hurt I truly was. After several run-ins with "the other woman," where I acted as if I had no clue what happened between them, something inside me finally snapped.

If we were in an open relationship, and he could make intimate friends without repercussions, then I wanted a friend of my own. I found an online portal that catered to such requests and created my profile. It didn't take me long to start chatting with a few guys, and one in particular especially caught my attention. He was extremely handsome, easy to talk to, and also married. Win, win for me because I had found what I wanted but also felt like this relationship would never go too far.

Surely he wouldn't take this too seriously because of his wife; I certainly didn't want anything serious because I didn't want to complicate further what was already complicated. Plus he lived six hours away, on the other side of Austin. Flawless plan. What could possibly go wrong?

In a very smug fashion, I told my husband about the website and the men I'd been chatting with. An implied "Fuck you for hurting me. Now you have to share me, too." He hardly reacted. There was a slight wince when I told him I'd created an account but then he went back to acting like it was a normal thing for his wife to admit she was looking for a side piece. He asked questions about the site, and whether or not I had chatted with anyone. Then the conversation dropped off and he and I both ignored the rip tide that was underlying the glass-like surface of our relationship. Until Mother's Day.

I received a text from the Austin guy, messaging to wish me a good day. Everything went awry as my husband finally allowed himself to feel the magnitude of the situation.

He shouted, "Why is he texting MY wife?! Doesn't he have his own to worry about?!"

My reply was cold and indifferent: "YOUR wife? If you were so worried about YOUR wife then maybe you should have kept it in your pants."

The heated exchanges continued for the next several months. Using our words as swords to jab at one another in purposeful revenge, creating emotional wounds that were far deeper than anything my physical body had experienced. By the time Thanksgiving came around I couldn't take the constant anxiety and tension anymore, so I reached out to the company I had previously worked for before the move to west Texas. They had a position in Austin and immediately offered it to me. Within two weeks of making the decision to leave, I'd found a place for me and our daughter to live. Over Thanksgiving break, she and I moved six hours away from the scene of the crime, leaving my husband behind to finish his degree alone.

We went back and forth for the next year, divided on whether or not to stay in our marriage. We both continued to see other people and fought so much it was as if we'd forgotten how to have a civilized conversation with one another. But by the time he came back in the Spring of 2011 to complete his student teaching, we were both remorseful and ready to make amends. He moved back in with me and our daughter and we attempted marriage counseling to bridge the gap in our relationship. But the damage had been done. I was resentful and angry and refused to forgive him. Blinded by stubborn pride, I dismissed his attempts at reconciliation and turned a cold shoulder to the man I once viewed as my soulmate. I was no longer the happy-go-lucky girl who had entered this marriage with a heart full of joy. I was cynical, resentful, and cold towards the man that stole my innocence. I wanted to be happy again, but I didn't know how to forgive him. The entire experience changed who I was at the core. The pain I was holding inside had turned into a vile poison that was raging through my veins with no means of escape.

So I created an escape. I reconnected with the Austin guy and began to secretly see him again, denying to my husband (and myself) that it was anything but casual. Our offices were five minutes apart and we got together several times a week. Every morning before I even logged into my work applications I was logging into messenger to say hello to him and catch up on how his evening was. We were not just lovers but also best friends, fully immersed in one another's lives behind closed doors. The affair was a nice departure from the reality I despised, and I depended on it for gratification.

Learning to Love

Somewhere under the surface of my vile behavior I knew what I was doing was wrong, but I still wasn't ready to condeede. There was a glitch in my machine that was triggered when someone would say to me "You can't do that." A switch would flip, blinding me to all rationality, and my immediate and instinctual response would be, *Yes I can. Watch me.* I felt like I was split into two personalities: the good church girl who was instilled with morals and the rebel archist who just didn't give a damn. The toll this internal battle was taking on my life forced me to evaluate my integrity. Not just in my marriage, but in everything I did. I was raised in a strong Christian home where there was no adultery during my parents forty years of marriage. Hell, my father didn't even allow alcohol or profanity in his presence. Infidelity was a foreign concept to me, and yet here I was smack dab in the middle of The Scarlet Letter.

After the pneumonia diagnosis and Reiki session in 2012, I began to unearth those core values from the pile of bullshit I had laid upon them. During that Reiki session it was as if I had exited my body and viewed my life from a higher perspective. I could see that how I had been living was destroying my soul and there was no future for me on my current path. On the drive home, I was in a complete daze. *What the hell just happened?* The shroud of indignity that had been clouding my vision was lifted and I offered myself the opportunity for a second chance. I knew I needed to quit this repressing lifestyle, but how would I do that? A: My family was dependent on my income. Because I only did massage part time, I didn't have much of a following, and starting a business from the ground up seemed like a pipe dream waiting to implode. And B: The thought of leaving my guy in Austin was gut wrenching. We had created a co-dependent relationship together and I wasn't sure I was strong enough to move on without it. But this new connection I had made with my inner self didn't care. She told me to trust. Use the stubborn will I was born with and make it happen.

And so I did. Two months later I'd quit my corporate job and said goodbye to my Austin boyfriend. My husband and I vowed to put our hearts full on into this new venture together and I signed a lease on an office space in an old, two-story Victorian house turned office building. It was close to home, and for the first time in my life I had the freedom to make a schedule that benefited both me and my family. The room I rented had the original wood floors that creaked when you walked and was at the bottom of a hand carved stairwell, a stark contrast to the cold gray walls of the corporate office I left behind. It was tiny, just big enough for one person to walk around a massage table. But I didn't care because it made me happy. It had an intricately carved fireplace with a patina mirror. As much as I loved that mirror, I was also cautious of looking into it too often. Worried that I was going to see one of the ghosts who reportedly haunted the house standing next to me, I usually avoided direct eye contact with the glass. I welcomed the idea of sharing my office with an unearthly visitor, I just didn't want to see them standing next to me as I massaged my clients.

I hadn't completely let go of the fear of starting my own business, but I put more energy into trusting and things quickly fell into place. Within a few months I was so busy that I had to hire a second therapist to help me cover all of the requests for massages. I began seeking out other modalities to enhance my practice and chose Reiki to be the first of many alternative healing methods I would learn over the years.

Because my personal experience with Reiki in 2012 had such a profound effect on me, I knew that it could help my clients as well. What I didn't realize at the time was how it would also enhance my personal life. This was the beginning of the evolution of my heart, the place where I began to learn how to weave love into everything I did. My dark night of the soul was coming to an end and I was finally able to see life from a place of gratitude.

Talking to Angels

In the five years following the launch of my business, I became like an over-ambitious sponge who was trying to soak up all of the water in the ocean. I took every alternative healing modality class I could sign up for. I learned all about the akashic records, astrology, tarot cards, shamanic practices, channeling, etc. I was super immersed in not only my own healing, but the healing of others.

For the first time in my life I felt like I was finally embracing who I am at the core, but something was still holding me back from fully acknowledging this newfound spiritual lifestyle. I knew it had been there all along, and I had always wanted to live the life of an intuitive healer, but there was still a deep inner fear of judgment. In order to be my most authentic self I needed to find out where that fear was coming from and rid it from my consciousness.

On what was supposed to be an anniversary trip to northern New Mexico in February 2017 that turned out to be a solo trip, I took on my own after my husband received word he would have to work that weekend. It was also my saving grace. I spent the weekend mostly alone, hiking, horseback riding, and just talking to

> In order to be my most authentic self I needed to find out where that fear was coming from and rid it from my consciousness.

God. On my last day at the retreat center I hiked up to the highest peak and decided to do a FaceBook live. The words about my journey poured out of me like someone had broken the faucet and there was no way to stop the flow. In this moment of complete vulnerability I finally received the answer to why I felt fear of judgment: my father. If I could gain acceptance for being an intuitive healer from this man, a devout Baptist Deacon, I wouldn't have anything left to fear. But how the hell would I even approach the subject of spirituality with him? The fear of talking to him was greater than the fear of anything else I could imagine. So I asked for divine guidance and trusted that when the time was right, I would know.

Somewhere amidst my personal journey of self-discovery, my father was diagnosed with cancer. His first round of chemo was tough, but he made it through and was declared cancer free after two years of horrific treatments. In January of 2017, it came back with a vengeance, this time in his brain. Within a short period of time he was having moments of detachment from our physical reality and believing he was safe at home rather than in a cold hospital bed. So, it was no surprise to me and my sister when he told us one day that he had seen an angel. But this time his storytelling was different. His mind was clear and he made perfect sense. He didn't want my mom to worry and only told us about it after she was out of the room. I sat, stunned, at his openness and honesty with us. In order for him to be this vulnerable this had to be something that shook him to the core. When my mother returned, it was clear that he had used my sister and I as guinea pigs to determine his level of confidence in telling my mom his experience. He opened up to her and said he had talked with us. He wanted to be honest with her as well. She accepted his story with love and compassion the same way my sister and I had. We all took a moment to process his story, and in the silence I could hear God in my ear, "Here's your chance."

So I said to him, "Dad, since we're all being honest here, there's something I need to tell you…If you want to know what the meaning of that experience was, I can tell you. Because I talk to angels."

He looked at me, blinked in confusion as he studied my words, and simply said "Yeah…?" Like, duh, okay get to the point. His immediate acceptance slapped me in the face. Why had I waited so long to tell him this? Of course he knew who I was. Just because we had different views on religion and spirituality didn't mean that he didn't love me and accept me for who I am. In that moment, I dropped all ideas of judgment and was able to have a beautiful conversation with him, opening me up to yet another level of love and acceptance.

He passed a few weeks later, and I am so grateful to have had the opportunity to finally be my true authentic self with the one person I held in the highest regard when it came to the full acceptance of who I am.

Amicable Divorce

After my father's passing things were profoundly better with my husband. The experience brought us closer together, and yet the new perspective on life pulled us farther apart. There was a renewed level of respect, but the passion had died long ago and we were living life together as roommates. He had his interests, I had mine. And every now and then we'd come together as husband and wife, then immediately return to feelings of indifference.

It was now May of 2017 and one Saturday morning we lay in bed talking about our lack of intimacy. He made the all too familiar comment to me, "I wish you were…" I don't recall what or who it was that he wished I was, but it didn't matter. He was still holding on to that girl I had been at the beginning of our relationship. The one that was free and wild. The one that worshiped and adored him. The one that wasn't jaded by the aftermath of an affair.

I wasn't her, nor would I ever be her again. It would seem an injustice to our experience if I regressed back to that person. Because of the self-reflecting work I had been doing, I was able to say to him, with all the love in my heart, "We shouldn't be together anymore." He was quiet for just a moment. Then just as calmly and confidently, he agreed. We spent the next few hours mapping out a timeline of what to do. We agreed that we would not tell anyone, especially the kids, until after school was out. My son was a senior in high school and was already greatly affected by my dad's death. We wanted this transition to be as smooth as possible for all affected parties.

We agreed that we were still going to be family and it was important to us that the kids never felt disjointed. We had already come through the ugly part and were no longer angry or resentful toward one another, we were just ready to move on. When he moved out in July, we made it a family affair. We shopped for furniture and housewares together. We moved his things together, and we even had dinner together at his apartment.

The Mastery Of Love

My husband and I were able to walk away from a fifteen-year marriage with minimal residual effects, and we continue to be friends today. I don't know that any of this would have been possible without the deep reflection work I had been doing. It paved a passage of forgiveness and love, making me want to be a better person and an example to everyone who comes across my path. And in that vein, I am determined to make sure my children don't suffer the same consequences I have and that they live a more authentic life from early on. I'm using my stubborn ways now as a means to create a beautiful reality, instead of destroying it.

It's said that the shaman is the wounded warrior who can only help others as much as they help themselves. Well, I'm still helping myself, and that's okay. I haven't stopped learning my lessons, and that's okay too. I look forward to what's next because I can look at it from a perspective of love. I no longer dread the unknown, but instead embrace it. That is, after all, what makes life exciting.

Mary Louise Lancaster

I'm Mary Louise Lancaster and I am so ecstatic to be here on the planet during this time of exponential soul growth.

I have come through many transformative events that led me to a place of understanding and compassion for others who were in the depths of their own darkness. This created a deep devotion to helping them find balance with the light and realizing their fullest potential.

I spent my twenties torn between higher education pursuits, a career in healthcare administration, raising babies, and trying to figure out who I was and why I couldn't find my happiness. In 2012, much to the protest of everyone I knew, I quit my corporate job to open a massage practice, Restful Waters.

Over the next ten years I studied many alternative modalities including Reiki, the Akashic Records, and Shamanic Breathwork. I was ordained as a Shamanic Minister with Venus Rising Association for Transformation in 2020 and my practice shifted completely from healing the physical body to healing the whole human experience. Through my practice, I not only embrace their greatness, but also empower them to go out and do the soul restoration work on their own. I am currently living out a dream to turn these teachings into books.

CONNECT WITH MARY

 solo.to/dlcollective

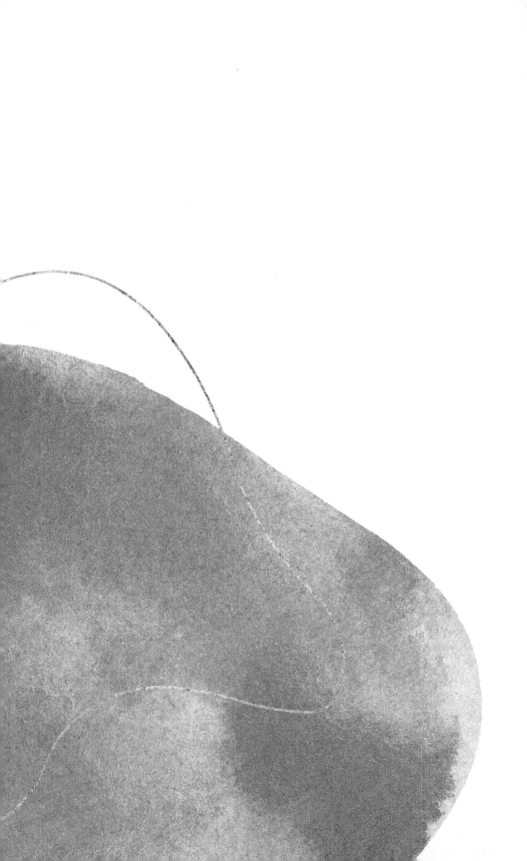

CHAPTER 7

Self-Loathing, Lust, and an STI:

HOW I FINALLY LEARNED TO LOVE MYSELF

By Christy (ChiChi) Yip

I wonder when he'll text me back.

I sat there at my desk, huddled under a fleece blanket, and bounced my leg uncontrollably. The desk trembled with me, causing the mug of tea to nearly splash all over the keyboard. I forced my leg to stop, as to not draw attention to myself. I pretended to write emails while sneaking glances at my phone with anticipation—the black mirror of the screen reflecting my face back to me.

I tapped the screen of my phone to check the time. Zero notifications. Zero messages. Zero news.

Losing my patience, I picked up my phone and scrolled through our text message conversation, reading into every detail of what was said. Everything seemed to be going so well. Where did it go wrong? I checked the timestamp of the last message I sent.

Yesterday at 8:54 pm.

Well, he was probably asleep when I texted, and a lot of people don't check their phones while they're at work during the day.

Except me. I checked my phone constantly throughout the day in between emails and conference calls, waiting for a text back.

Maybe if I send energetic vibes his way he will text me back. Or maybe if I stop thinking about it he will text back.

Except I couldn't stop thinking about it. My mind kept making up stories and speculating about what he was doing, why he wasn't looking at his phone, and why he wasn't responding. I read through our conversation again and again, replaying it in my head.

Shit, did I text too soon? Maybe I should've waited thirty more minutes to not seem desperate. Or maybe I should've waited two more days before responding. Maybe he's waiting to not seem desperate.

I hated playing games. These days, you're supposed to pretend not to care in order to attract someone and get them to chase after you. Isn't that totally counterintuitive? I prefered straightforward honesty because honesty is the best policy, right? Except honesty would always repel people and scare them away. Maybe guys don't like it when women come off too strong. They live for the chase—it's in their nature. This was a pattern that kept repeating itself over and over again.

Perhaps I was insane. I was insane for doing this to myself again and again. Each time I met someone new, I fooled myself into thinking that maybe this time he'll be different.

Why did I always act like a fool when it came to men? I continually lowered my standards, accepted terrible treatment, became desperate, and came off too strong. I chased after people who didn't want me, screaming PICK ME PICK ME PICK ME.

"The definition of insanity is doing the same thing over and over again and expecting a different result."

– ALBERT EINSTEIN

I was a hopeless romantic. I hoped to meet someone who would find something to love about me. I hoped that someone would pick me because I had all the traits that anyone would want in a partner. I would be the greatest love they ever had! So why didn't anyone choose me?

That's because I didn't love myself. I loathed myself. What I didn't realize until later was being in love with myself was all I ever needed.

You know what they say. You will experience the same situation over and over again until you learn your lesson. Usually, the lesson is learned the hard way.

And I sure did. Before I could learn this lesson, I had to endure a lot of pain throughout my life. Something drastic needed to happen—a major wake up call to slap the sense into me. What I thought was the most painful moment in my life turned out to be the greatest lesson.

> What I thought was the most painful moment in my life turned out to be the greatest lesson.

● ● ●

The self-loathing started at a young age. I was a chubby kid with undesirable physical features—or at least that's what I was taught to believe. I never saw anyone that looked like me in movies and magazines. Every starlet I watched on the silver screen was thin, pretty, and caucasian. The models in magazines all had straight, white teeth; perfectly arched brows; long, curly lashes; and big, bright eyes. As opposed to me with my protruding jaw, sparse eyebrow hairs, toothpick-straight lashes, and crescent moon eyes. My features were not considered beautiful by anyone—so why would I believe that I was beautiful?

My differences were made even more prominent by contrast to the girls I was surrounded by in school. When you are one of a few Asian girls in the room, you start to wonder if there's something wrong with you because you look nothing like the people surrounding you. One time on the playground in first grade, a girl in thick, prescription glasses squinted her eyes at me and asked, "How can you see?" My vision was perfect—20/20 vision. However it was true—I couldn't see the beauty in my uniqueness.

I have a vivid memory of myself leaving school, sitting in the back of my mom's eggplant-purple minivan and praying that I would be reincarnated in the next life as a white girl with blonde hair and blue eyes. Because if I did, then I would be happy and free of any problems. I didn't want to be me. I wished I could be someone else.

I was self-conscious about my weight for as long as I can remember. I don't know if there was ever a day that went by when I wasn't thinking about the size of my body and how it took up more space than others. I first noticed that I was bigger than the girls in ballet class. I was only seven years old. When you spend hours dancing in front of a mirror wearing skin-tight leotards standing next to girls that are much thinner than you, it becomes very apparent that you are on the larger side of the spectrum for children under ten. The other girls were like elegant swans with long, thin limbs and svelte torsos. I was shaped like a stubby penguin with my short, thick legs and round belly. My thighs didn't touch, my back wasn't bony, and my ribs didn't stick out from under my chest like theirs. There wasn't a hollow space where my stomach was, no matter how much I sucked in.

The size of my body was underscored when I would go to family gatherings and relatives I hadn't seen in many years would make comments.

"You've gotten *so* big," they would say.

They didn't mean it as in, "wow, you're growing up."

They meant it as in, "wow, you're so fat."

I became increasingly self-conscious about my weight. I was only a young girl, still growing and learning about the world and who she was. So much of these years were riddled with intrusive thoughts about my body and how much I hated being a fat girl.

The self-hatred and body dysmorphia continued into my teens and into my twenties. I spent hours staring in the mirror at my reflection and obsessing about the parts that I wanted to change about myself. I thought that if I lost weight around my waist and my hips, maybe my hip bones would protrude like the girls I would see in fashion magazines. My scapula would poke out of my back and you could see each vertebra through my spine. Those were my body goals. Those were the features I thought were beautiful.

I spent as much time obsessing over my body as I did daydreaming about falling in love. Just like in the Disney movies, I wished that one day my prince would come. Being loved by someone was all I ever wanted. If somebody loved me, then that would mean that I am accepted. That I am loveable. That I am worthy. That I am enough. My prince would save me, and all my problems would go away. Much to my dismay, my prince never came.

As I entered junior high, all my friends were getting boyfriends.

Except for me.

I was never chosen.

I was never asked to the school dances.

What was wrong with me?

Was it because I was fat? Was it because I was ugly? Was it because I was Asian?

I never had a boyfriend in high school. I had plenty of crushes, but all of them were unrequited. Anytime I would confess my crush to a friend, they would steal them away. I was the ugly duckling - rejected and ostracized from everyone else. Nobody would ever want to choose me, and nobody would ever want to love me.

The weeks after I graduated high school, on a typical hot summer night in Texas where the dense air clung to your skin and lungs, somebody noticed me for the first time. We sat across from each other on the patio table in my friend's backyard as we passed around joints and cracked jokes. I said something that made everyone around the table erupt in laughter.

After the giggles settled down, his green eyes looked directly into mine and he said, "You're very charming."

I blushed and felt a spark—a little tingling flame that ignited a scintillation inside me like nothing I'd ever felt before. Nobody had ever said anything like that about me.

From that night on, we started dating. I had never met anyone who had seen me for me—who liked me for me. He melted my heart like the heat wave that scorched across Texas in June. The little girl inside who only wanted to be loved finally felt whole and complete. The little girl who believed in true love finally got everything she ever wanted. He was my first love, and I was starting to think that he was the one.

We spent the rest of summer in the honeymoon phase where everything seemed easy, blissful, and seamless. As summer came to a close and my first semester of college loomed ahead, reality started to sink in. We went to school three hours apart in New York, and decided to make a long-distance relationship work. We knew that a long distance relationship would be challenging, and we would be required to make many sacrifices. But for me, it was worth it for the love I had been searching for all of my life. I was willing to put my heart on the line and my trust in his hands. My trust that he ultimately broke.

After my freshman year of college, our relationship took a turn. He became someone different—someone I didn't recognize. There was a darkness about him that I never saw coming. He would say terrible things about his mother and he refused to return to school to finish his final year of university. Everything he worked for, all the potential he had, he threw out the window.

Despite all of that, I wasn't ready to throw it all away. Despite all of that, I stayed. Even after being cheated on. Even after being manipulated and gaslit. I stayed. I stayed because I steadfastly believed in true love. I stayed because I believed that love could overcome any obstacle because love transcends all, so I overlooked all the flaws and the red flags. At that age, I did not know what love was. I did not know who I was. I was foolish and naive, and he knew to take advantage of it.

When he decided not to return to New York to finish college, the relationship ended, and I experienced heartbreak for the first time. What they say is true—the first cut really is the deepest. After the breakup, I viewed love in an entirely different way. I didn't believe in it anymore, and I became cynical. I thought I would never recover. I thought I would never be the same. When your heart is shattered, it feels like it will be impossible to ever love again.

What does one usually do after a break up? (Aside from eating ice cream and crying in bed.) They rebound. They find something to fill the void. I rebounded hard. I bounced around hoping to be picked up by the next player. A newly single Christy returning to her sophomore year of college—anything was possible. Enter: the slut era number 1.

I was desperate to find a way to piece myself back together and find myself again. I needed to prove to myself and the world that I was still loveable. That I was still desirable. Except I was looking in all the wrong places. I wasn't looking for love—I was looking for validation. I believed that being found attractive by men was what defined my worth. It became a numbers game for me. How many men could I attract and ensnare with my charm?

Our culture is so obsessed with sex that we are defined by how much sex we are having and how often we are having it. Our generation places our value on how sexually desirable you are. The number of people you sleep with defines who you are as a person. If you are having sex, that means you are valuable.

I took that and ran with it. I needed to feel worthy again. My dorm room was like a revolving door. I started keeping a tally in my little black book. I felt accomplished. I felt like I was achieving something great by seducing men. At the end of the day, no matter how many trysts I had, I was lonely.

These cycles would continue through my twenties. Your twenties are supposed to be all about exploration, experimentation, and self-discovery. You spend this decade figuring out who you are and how you fit into the world. Most of my identity was discovered through going out and partying, and San Francisco was the prime place for that. Some call it Neverland, because the adults that live here never want to grow up, just like Peter Pan and the Lost Boys. There was all the fun in the world to be had in the 7x7 mile city by the bay.

Twenty-seven was the year my partying peaked. That age is the perfect (and dangerous) intersection of having a decent amount of responsibility but not too much, and having more disposable income to play around with but no big expenses. This was also the time when I built my closest friendships and bonded over bottles of tequila, staying up until sunrise in a friend's living room, chain smoking cigarettes in the backyard trying to keep our voices down so as to not upset the neighbors. Everything about life seemed perfect and the world was my oyster. I was having all the fun in the world—dressing up in elaborate outfits and going to theme parties every weekend. San Francisco was my playground—the backdrop of the circus that was my life.

I felt like I was finally in a good, stable place in my life. My rent was cheap. I was earning the most income I've ever made at a company that I enjoyed working at. My circle of friends was growing and the bonds were getting stronger. My Saturn return was right around the corner, and for the first time in my life, I was feeling confident about the direction I was going in.

On the surface, life was working out great for me. I had everything anyone could ever want. A good career, amazing friends, and living in a wonderful, rent-controlled apartment in one of the greatest cities in the world. Except, deep down below, I was unhappy. I was extremely insecure. Internally, I was battling the negative self-talk that was constantly looming over me—reminding me that I wasn't shit. The inner critic that lived in my head rent-free and berated me day in and day out.

Nobody knew that something was wrong with me because I hid it so well. I've always been skilled at hiding my true feelings from other people, especially myself. A master of deception. What a lot of people didn't know about me was that I was still hurting from the end of my last relationship. The relationship was with the second person I ever fell in love with. A year had already passed since it ended, yet my heart was still in recovery.

This heartbreak was different from the first in that we ended because of distance. When you're on the other side of the world from your love, the only cause of a breakup is the circumstance. Nothing was wrong with him or me, except for where we lived. We loved each other dearly and truly, but we were in the wrong place, wrong time. For me, this was the most painful way of breaking up. When someone wrongs you or hurts you, it's easier to sever those emotions and move on. But when the love is still there, it's even harder to release and heal. My heart yearned for the love we shared, and the grieving lingered because I was unable to let go of what we had.

When we were together, I was drinking less because he disliked alcohol. I was usually sober with him, and I was a better version of myself because of him. After our relationship ended, I returned to my old habit of drinking to drown out my pain and my sadness. I went back to partying to numb myself from the loneliness and heartbreak. I became self-destructive and slowly declined into the worst version of myself.

During this time, I gained a lot of excess weight. The type of weight gain that is so gradual that you never notice the changes in your body until you're forced to look. When I was confronted by my reflection in the mirror, I was appalled by what I saw reflecting back at me. I struggled to button my jeans over my hips and belly. I pulled up my waistband as high as I could to hide the muffin top that spilled over the top of my pants. My face was bloated from the alcohol and tears. I looked and felt miserable. How did I allow myself to become like this? I became the thing that I've detested my whole life and fought hard to change.

My hatred of my body brewed while I kept searching for external validation. I turned to alcohol and drugs because when I was drunk and high, I couldn't hear my inner critic that was constantly whispering negative words in my ear.

"You're fat and disgusting."

"How could you do this to yourself? You are a failure."

"Nobody is going to love you when you look like that."

The alcohol would silence those voices.

The alcohol was a distraction. When I drank, I could feel happy and exist freely and blissfully. I was flirtatious, fun, and unabashed.

The alcohol was a crutch. When I drank, I could act silly without worrying about judgment and if I ever did anything stupid, I could blame it on the alcohol. The only thing I worried about was when and what I would drink next.

But the alcohol was a troublemaker. When I drank, I would sometimes end up in dangerous situations. I would do things against my better judgment because it was impaired.

On a Thursday night before a long weekend, I went out to the club to see a popular local DJ. Everyone from the San Francisco dance music scene was there that night. Because of the special occasion of a rare Friday morning where I could sleep in, I celebrated by having a few extra tequila sodas with lime. The additional tequilas gave me the courage to dance up to a guy and draw him in with my charms. It was an easy catch, and perhaps not a quality one. A mediocre fish in the sea. But that didn't matter to me.

I said goodbye to my friends, stumbled into the back of a car and cozied up in my fur coat next to someone I had just met. I had zero recollection of his name and zero clue as to where we were heading. Honestly, I forgot and honestly, I wasn't going to ask because I probably would never see him again.

My brain throbbed inside of my skull and my tongue stuck to the roof of my mouth as I started to come to my senses. I could taste the lingering effects of too much tequila soda with lime. I felt immediate regret. I needed to get out of there before it got too late. I scrambled around his bedroom, feeling around the floor for my clothes amongst the messy piles on the floor. I got dressed hastily, avoiding his gaze.

"Okay, my car's here I gotta go."

That was a lie. I hadn't even called a car yet. I just needed to get out and did not want to exchange information. As I ran out the door, I rubbed my fingers under my eyes to remove the smudged mascara on my face.

A few weeks later, I woke up with painful bumps in my nether region. I knew something was wrong, but I was in denial so I searched on the internet to diagnose myself.

"They're just ingrown hairs," I told myself. "I get them all the time, it'll go away soon."

Except the pain didn't go away, and it only got worse. So I did what had to be done—I had to go to the doctor to find out for certain.

I waited in the examination room in complete silence, alone, the bottom half of my body wrapped in a thin paper gown. I studied the anatomical posters of uteruses and penises on the wall, reading them to keep my mind occupied. Fluorescent lights glared over my head.

I shivered. Why do they insist on making the doctor's office feel like the freezer section of a grocery store?

Two doctors entered the room.

"Lay back and put your feet up in the stirrups."

I laid there on the stiff examination table with my legs propped up by two stirrups. It was so considerate of them to put socks on the foot holders to keep me cozy in this most uncomfortable situation. My knees kept instinctively knocking together as I attempted to relax.

"Scoot your butt closer to the edge, please."

I shimmied one centimeter closer to the edge of the examination table.

"Closer."

My knees were nearly up to my chest.

"There. Okay you can relax."

I could not relax. I felt vulnerable and exposed. I wanted to dissociate.

I have opened my legs so easily for strangers—how was this any different?

The doctors examined me down there, prodding me with cotton swabs.

The room was cold but I was sweating. The clammy skin on my back began sticking to the crepe paper lining on the table. I stared up at the drop ceiling—frozen. If I stared long enough, maybe I could disappear.

The doctors looked at each other and nodded.

They said my test results would be back within two-three days, gave me pamphlets about birth control and STIs, and sent me on my way.

Those days felt like an eternity. I incessantly refreshed my email to see if there were any updates on my fate.

What was a routine message for them felt like a death sentence to me. Three letters that would take me to my final resting place.

HSV1 - Positive

My stomach dropped like a brick. A rush of heat rose up the back of my neck and into my ears, and I felt the ground fall from under me.

My brain couldn't comprehend it. This wasn't really happening to me. How could that be possible? I was being safe. I used protection. I thought I was protected.

That's what always happens though, right? We play stupid games and when we fly a little too close to the sun, we promise we won't make the same mistake twice. Sometimes life can be a sick joke because even when you think you're doing better, you still win stupid prizes.

In that moment, I knew that my sex life would be over and I would never touch another human again. No one will ever want to come near me. I was tainted.

The shame. Shame hurts us the most. Shame is the lowest level of human consciousness—and I never thought I could ever rise from it.

The stigma. Nobody wants to be intimate with someone who has herpes. I could never tell anyone because I know what people think about herpes. It's always the butt of the joke. Only dirty people get it and once you have it, you're an abomination of humanity. You're no longer a human that is deserving of love and respect.

The fear of rejection caused me to push everyone away. I stopped dating. I stopped talking to any men. I crawled into my hole because I never wanted to see the light of day ever again. For months, I stayed buried in my shame. The girl who was once outgoing and fun-loving lost her spark.

I spent most of my life hating my body and fighting against it, and now I was revolted by it. Repelled by it. Whatever fraction of an ounce of self-esteem I had left was entirely gone—flushed away like tears in the rain. My ego, crushed under the unbearable weight of a herpes diagnosis. I was permanently stained.

What did I do to deserve this? I was a good person. Perhaps I was a bit misguided by my ego, but all I wanted was to be loved. Who would love me now? I felt alone.

But I wasn't alone. I connected with people who were living with the same condition and were unbothered by it. Herpes wasn't a big deal to them. I couldn't comprehend it at the time because I felt so much shame and fear of rejection. They were living their lives. They were dating, in serious relationships, having casual sex—all the things that seemed like a far away dream to me was a reality for them. They were thriving.

The more I learned about the condition, the more I understood the truth about it. Everything I thought I knew about herpes was wrong. The

The more I healed, more was revealed.

reality of herpes is that the stigma is worse than the actual condition itself. I was guilty of stigmatizing herpes and treating it like a horrendous disease that only the dirtiest of the scum of the earth would ever have. If I believed that about herpes, then what does that mean about me, a person who has herpes?

More than half the population has herpes, and so many people are unaware that they do.

I realized I couldn't hide forever. I needed to heal in order to continue living my life. I turned this into an opportunity to shift my focus on myself and embarked on a healing journey.

Once I started to peel back the layers, I uncovered everything that I needed to heal from. I was forced to face the darkest parts of my soul and confront my demons. From my damaged relationship with my body image, to the sexual assaults I survived, and the little girl inside me who just wanted to be loved. All of this pain that was ignored came bubbling to the surface and laid before me to reconcile.

The more I healed, more was revealed. I realized what needed to be done—I needed to learn to love myself.

So I became dedicated to cultivating my relationship myself and became intentional with every aspect of my life. I learned about how to take care of my health. I studied nutrition so I could nourish my body with the right food. I exercised because I liked the way it made me feel. I transformed my relationship with my body and accepted it. I became sober and stopped hurting myself. I connected with my higher self and healed my inner child. I leaned into the activities that brought me the most joy and followed my bliss. Every step that I took on my journey, even if it was two steps forward and one step back, I was slowly unveiling my true self that I was hiding from all this time.

One day, while looking at my reflection in the mirror, something shifted. What would normally devolve into nitpicking and obsessing over everything I wished were different, I decided instead to look beyond the physical. What I saw staring back at me was a strong woman who experienced so much pain in her lifetime and still rose above. I saw a caring, compassionate woman who is loyal to her loved ones and dedicated to helping others. I saw my ancestors and the generations of women who came before me. I saw my divinity and the miracle that is life on this earth.

I felt empowered. I felt confident. I felt indestructible. I felt more sure about who I was and what I stood for in the world. I knew who I was at my core, and it was someone worthy of love. I was in love with the version of myself I was becoming.

● ● ●

This was the turning point in the trajectory of my entire life. What I believed would be the end of my life actually ended up saving my life. If this never happened, I would have continued down the same self-destructive path of self-loathing. I would still be deeply insecure, seeking validation from others. I would still settle for less than what I deserved and accept terrible treatment from men. I would still be unhappy, looking for the solution outside of me. I would still be chasing the dragon, riding the never-ending hedonic rollercoaster. I could finally step off and step into my power.

Herpes ended up being my greatest teacher. This didn't happen to me—this happened FOR me. After everything that I went through, after everything that happened, what I realized is that being in love with myself was all I ever needed.

Continuing on my life path, I've taken what I've learned through my experiences and turned it into my soul's purpose: helping women fall in love with themselves. This had to happen for me so I could show others the light. There is no greater blessing than to inspire women to love themselves fully, because we all deserve to love ourselves.

And now, in this present moment, sharing my story that I've been afraid to share. However, sharing my story is the most courageous action I can take. It is the final step in my healing process because it will help others realize that they can heal, too.

Christy Yip

Hello, my name is Christy Yip. You can call me ChiChi.

And yes, I know what that means in Spanish.

I spent five years working in the nonprofit sector and four years at a tech start-up before the universe kicked my butt to the curb and forced me to question my purpose on this earth. After listening to spirit and my stomach, I was called to study holistic nutrition. I received my Holistic Nutrition Certification from Bauman College in Berkeley, CA in 2020.

I am now a self-proclaimed Self-Love Empowerment Coach, focused on body and food freedom. I help women transform their relationship with their body and food so they can love themselves and manifest what they deserve. I am the host of the podcast, 'The Sistriarchy Sessions,' where we talk about topics like self-love, social issues, spiritual growth, and personal development.

Fueled by love and compassion, I am called to do this work because of my desire to subvert the patriarchal paradigm that we are forced to live under. My vision is to build a thriving and just society that is created by the collective for the collective.

CONNECT WITH CHRISTY

 @chichi_lovesyou  solo.to/chichi_lovesyou

CHAPTER 8

My Work vs. My Purpose

By Chotsani Sackey

Opening

I was looking forward to that Wednesday morning. No, I wasn't going to the beach or to a day spa, I was having a procedure I originally thought would happen in September. Fortune would have it that I wouldn't have to carry my discomfort through my summer birthday celebration—because I celebrate the WHOLE month of August! Today, I knew no one would be able to reach me. No calling or emailing me. No child; no colleagues. I'd be left alone, with someone else taking care of my physical needs—while I was anesthetized. This hospital stay would double as a mental health time-out. "Here's some oxygen, Ms. Sackey. Just breathe and relax." I knew when I awakened there would be a huge sense of relief; pain, relief and healing were ahead.

Four years ago today, I ascended. I became a Sacred Woman. I knew everything would work out.

It's Personal

At age fourteen, through my academic scholarship and achievement, I moved from public to private school. My daily surroundings changed from densely populated neighborhoods made up of rows of apartment buildings, to a select community of mansions, sprawling detached houses, manicured lawns, lush trees, and secluded roads. A private bus company transported many of my classmates to school, while others of us took local buses. This was the backdrop to my coming of age as a soon-to-be fatherless teenage girl. About six months into my adjustment to the social, cultural, academic, and environmental shift, my father passed away from an illness. He hadn't denied or abandoned me, but he had transitioned to another place and I couldn't go with him.

I couldn't ask Daddy adolescent questions about how boys communicate, how one should treat me on a date, or what qualities make a good boyfriend. Should he be tall and cute? Or funny and smart? All the above, perhaps? What was I supposed to look for? Who was I supposed to compare him to? How was I supposed to get him to notice me? According to my single-mothered upbringing, those were irrelevant questions. I was to go to school to get a good education and prepare for college. Growing up with Seventh-Day Adventist teachings, no interest was allowed to be put on ear piercings or makeup, let alone boys. Although I did wear uncomfortable clip-on earrings, and clear but not-too-shiny lip gloss, any attention I got from boys was deemed inappropriate and unnecessary to further my purpose as a student. Occasional nail-polish was kept to the clearest shade of pink on medium-length nails, otherwise I'd end up on the fast-hussy side of the girlhood-scale. Boys were trouble and would take me away from reaching the appropriate goal of graduating.

My social development would have to be vicarious through observation of and storytelling from friends. Dating at the age of sixteen was out of the question. There was no way I was going to be left alone, outside of school, without supervision, with a boy. Hanging out in a mixed company setting wasn't safe either. Boys and men were predators on shy and naive girls. These opinions and rulings were handed down to me as facts and laws. I had no counterarguments, because I had no life experience, nor permission to get any. Most significantly, my subject matter expert had passed away.

At seventeen, I graduated, and I was proud of myself, as were my mom, sister, grandpa, and of course, my dad up in heaven. My grandpa (dad's dad) had traveled to New York City all the way from the Virgin Islands to represent the Sackey clan. That summer, my sister graduated from law school, and I graduated from high school within days of each other. In the fall, as I headed off to an out-of-state college, that inner voice of caution followed me, warning me I needed to focus solely on academics and picking a major that was going to help me get a good job, assuming I didn't go straight into graduate school.

Progress was linear, so my goals had to be achieved one at a time. But I noticed some of my college friends had boyfriends who would later turn into spouses. Many are still married to this day. They *also* are professionally successful. They also have families. Looking back, it is interesting and thought-provoking to realize I was surrounded by so many peers who seemed to be successfully balancing and achieving their academic and life goals. I recall feeling like there must be a secret recipe and I was missing ingredients. What was more likely was I didn't know basic rules to the game of life, because I wasn't aware I was playing a game. Further analysis revealed most of my closest college peers had grown up in two-parent households, or had both parents still alive; and some had opposite sex siblings. My peers' conditions provided them the advantage of role models and coaches for dealing with intimate relationships. Apparently, these advantages had bypassed me.

I approached college graduation in a state of excitement, confusion, frustration, jealousy, impatience, and young-adult angst. Now, what? I consulted my mental list of goals, worked as a paralegal for two years, and then went to law school. This was supposed to be my endgame. My adolescent social life sacrifices for the pursuit of academic success were supposed to lead to a career that would set me up financially for life.

Since I was assured by family and friends that being in a relationship was inevitable, I naively thought I just had to be patient, because those relationship skills would organically and magically hone themselves. I would be able to relax and settle down, and live my life while starting my professional career. Up to this point, I had made all the right life choices, and stayed out of trouble. The return on my investment surely was coming. But alas, by the time law school graduation rolled around, I had neither a job nor a life-mate lined up.

The devastation of September 11th had occurred two years prior, and the subsequent recession left many employers cautious about shelling out quarter-of-a-million-dollar annual salaries to as many incoming candidates as they had in previous years. Worse yet, I hadn't passed either the New York or New Jersey bar exams on the first, second, or third tries. The realization of not being self-sufficient and having to move back home after achieving my highest academic-to-professional honor sent me straight into therapy.

I spent many of my early years in therapy trying to cope with the feeling of "why me?" Based on how I was feeling, I defined my reality as being stuck, embarrassed, betrayed, and subjected to punishment for some unknown, perhaps karmic, reason. That was not the ideal emotional state of mind for dating, pursuing a healthy relationship, laying the foundation for creating a family, let alone, shaping my entry into motherhood.

From Disappointment to Surprise: Part 1

I'd stopped attending social events, high school, and college reunions while I was waiting to pass the bar. I'd ceased going to happy hours, movies, and dinners with friends and family. I opted out because the vicious cycle of studying for the bar exam and awaiting results was tiring. The exam is only offered twice a year, in February and July. The February test cast a shadow over the new beginnings promised in spring. The fun, rest, and relaxation of summer and fall were dampened by the waiting period for the July results. Those results were usually released right before Thanksgiving. You knew whether or not you passed based upon the size and thickness of the mail you received. Inside the envelope was either a congratulatory letter or a breakdown of your scores and shortfalls. The anxiety this caused me was coupled with inconsistent and unpredictable access to cash flow associated with working sporadic, hourly temp jobs. My social calendar was cleared because disposable income was at a bare minimum, or non-existent.

When catching up with extended family around the holidays, invariably they wanted to know all about the new developments in my life. I was tired of discussing how I felt about not passing, whether my scores were going up, and whether I knew how to improve for the next time. I also told myself I didn't deserve to have fun until I passed. If I didn't study, take practice tests, and analyze why I hadn't passed, I would miss a clue, and wouldn't pass again. In linear mode, without a law license, I wouldn't get a desirable job, or make a good living. I didn't allow myself to think of anything other than passing the test. Therefore, I wouldn't allow myself to set any other goals until that was accomplished.

After I surpassed my sixth time taking the bar, I stopped tracking progress and looking for patterns in my failures. I continued to take the test just once a year until I finally told myself, "If I don't pass the bar the next time I take it, I'm not taking it again! I'll have to figure out something else to do with my life!" I was sick of riding the see-saw motion of getting my hopes up followed by steep disappointment and embarrassment. I didn't want to hear anymore recounted stories of successful or infamous attorneys who didn't pass on the first try, and now had great jobs or careers. The pep talks about how admirable my perseverance and persistence were became more irritating. None of those sentiments helped me save for a down payment on a house or pay my student loans.

Enough was enough.

Then, lo and behold, more than six years after graduating from law school, I passed! THANK. GOD. What a relief! A few months later I was sworn in, enabling me to join the ranks of New York State licensed attorneys. I was finally legit!

And my therapy sessions continued.

My Limiting Beliefs Kept Me Grounded

About a year later, I was still single, living in my fancy new co-op apartment. I was still pondering why I felt like I had to pass that test before I could resume living. Why did I feel like I had to be professionally established before I could start a relationship? I needed to peel back those layers.

This linear and limiting belief structure kept me stuck in an inferior state of mind, such as one who was always reaching for the future good. I wasn't clearly seeing the present good: I had passed the New Jersey bar a few years earlier, been sworn in, and was

Why did I feel like I had to be professionally established before I could start a relationship?

already working in New York as an out-of-state licensed attorney. I still felt small, stagnant, and unaccomplished. Not the best face to put forward while trying to meet a special someone.

Throughout the rest of my thirties, I went along with the platitudes thrust upon me such as, "Save yourself for the one," "It's not your time yet," and "Maybe that's not for you." "That" being a life with my partner or my husband. Maybe I was destined to be the one "single friend" within my group of married sister-friends. My dating criteria was simple: *Can I see myself married to him? Do I want to have his children?*

Fast approaching my fortieth birthday, I was feeling pressure imposed by myself and society to be anything but single. I attended numerous baby showers, bridal showers, weddings, and first birthday parties. I was no longer eager to show my still single, not pregnant, no-engagement-ring-wearing self at these get-togethers. I was genuinely happy for my friends and family and their personal milestones. I was glad they had invited me to celebrate with them. However, my ongoing inner shame and self-judgment were causing an unhealthy, emotional swirl within me.

More platitudes addressed the status of my professional growth. "Be happy you have a job" or "At least you're working" were often recited to me to remind me I should be grateful because I was more fortunate than others. I would feel guilty about not being satisfied and wanting more for myself. I stopped sharing my feelings.

Anger and resentment had been simmering for over a decade. From the age of twenty-six, I watched my friends and classmates become professionally successful—accumulating well-deserved labels, titles, and accolades—while I remained unlicensed and unable to practice law for so long. Finally, I landed a job I enjoyed and was good at. My resentment of my circumstances started to dissipate.

The financial gains I expected were few and far between. I focused on my career and on getting equitable salary recognition while I waited to meet my life partner. So far it had been a long wait. Establishing myself professionally had been the prerequisite. The messages I received all led to the conclusion I had to be a whole package of success before I presented myself to the world as someone ready for a partner.

I was trained to be independent, responsible, and self-sufficient just in case my future, hypothetical relationship didn't work out. I was conditioned to plan for the contingency of surviving without a partner, rather than learn how to build a life with one. I was confused by the conflicting messages.

After a few more years, I landed a permanent job in the private sector, and carved out a viable career path, not just a short-term job option. Just as I was settling into my role and approaching the completion of year two, I was laid off.

I. Could. Not. Have. Been. More. Pissed.

I found out I was soon-to-be-unemployed when I went to work one Monday morning and the security guard greeted me with his usual, "Good Morning!" Then he asked where my office would be located when my company moved out in a couple weeks. (Wait, what?!) "Who's moving?" I asked. "You must be mistaken; we're not moving," I said to him. After a pause, he replied, "Oh, well, last week your boss said…." I didn't hear anything else after that as the elevator arrived and I rode up to my office. My mind spun with thoughts of, *What the hell is he talking about?* Later that morning, my boss' boss called me to deliver the bad news, that yes, our office was closing, but no, we weren't moving. I would be out of work in two weeks, including that Monday.

Here began my spiral into financial setbacks. I had to return to short-term employment. I wouldn't be making enough to pay my mortgage, co-op maintenance fees, cable, student loans, Metrocard, cell phone bills. What about my groceries? Unemployment benefits received in between temporary jobs could only subsidize—not sustain me. My legal career, already delayed before I was licensed, was stalled again. Exceeding the allotted deferment and forbearance periods, I was worried about paying my law school debt. I was preoccupied with getting a return on my academic investment. Simultaneously, I feared never receiving recognition for my professional accomplishments because my life had become out of sync with the professional lives of my graduating class peers.

I called it quits on strategically rotating which bills I would pay every other month. Trying to work out agreements to keep my apartment, with both my co-op board and the bank holding my mortgage, was a battle I lost. With my previous income, my monthly payments had been affordable. I would have paid off my mortgage early. Now I was faced with a bankruptcy and two dueling creditors who salivated while trying to reclaim the sanctuary I had created and custom-designed. Damn it!

I deserved to have a nice home. The wood blinds, granite countertops, and backsplash, ceramic and African slate tiles, recessed lighting, walk-in closets, remodeled bathroom and kitchen, were the culmination of my hard work and persistence, and represented my vision of comfort and security. After seven short years, I was slapped in the face with the realization this type of investment was feasible only for as long as I was gainfully employed by someone else. A situation out of my control. It settled in the pit of my stomach that my home was no longer mine when the bank representative called to confirm my move out date and remind me I had to vacate the premises and turn over my keys. Even though I had just secured a permanent job, it was too late. There were too many arrears, and I had broken my contracts.

On paper I looked unreliable. I was going to be a renter again and I thought, *Who would rent to me?* Luckily, my new income met a magic formula of eligibility. Using new-math calculations I didn't quite understand, I was able to rent an apartment. Ironically, the monthly rent was more than what my combined mortgage and maintenance had been for the apartment I lost.

The therapy continued.

Why? Why me? I was consumed by the need for answers to every predicament I was in. Why did I have to start my career late? Why did I have to lose my home? Why wasn't I happily partnered yet? No one could tell me that in all the couples I knew, each member had their respective shit together before they got married, or started dating. Why did I have to wait? I was resentful of having to go through these tribulations all alone, having no one to grow through them with. Having no emotional support. But since I was the common denominator in all these scenarios, my life was my responsibility, and I had to solve my own problems. Something was either wrong with the world, me, my approach, or my perspective. The world, I couldn't control.

Many self-help books later, it was time for some serious soul-searching. I chose to take a look at my point of view of the world and of myself. It was time to put on my big-girl-panties and get philosophical and introspective.

From Observing to Healing

For me, femininity was not a goal. It just was. It was obvious. I had nothing to prove. The same way I was Black, I didn't have to shape the context. It was a given. I personally didn't separate being a Black girl from being feminine. I didn't question it.

Femininity was not something I thought about until I went away to college. One of my new friends suggested I get colored contacts instead of wearing glasses. If I had to keep the glasses, another friend suggested I upgrade my appearance by plucking and shaping my eyebrows. Wearing more fitted clothing was another suggestion, but nothing too provocative. My internal voice of caution returned and reminded me, I was not in school to be judged by my looks or compete for male attention. Furthermore, I was a feminist. I was in college to set myself up for better access to graduate school, while protesting socio-economic discrimination and prejudice, politically advocating for equal treatment, pay and rights for women (particularly women of color), and questioning traditional gender and family roles. This coming of age as a young adult woman was set against the backdrop of the Million Woman March of 1997. We wanted to empower and unify ourselves in sisterhood, and rebuild the Black family unit and neighborhoods that had been systematically infiltrated and destroyed in the U.S.

Certain aspects of feminism landed differently for me because Black women, who had always worked, were not necessarily looking for equal access to work, or to be included in the male-dominated workforce. We were working, usually out of necessity rather than choice, to support our families and communities, often prioritizing the needs of humanizing our race over the needs of equalizing our gender. We didn't have the luxury of achieving social status via our husbands or fathers. Femininity and feminine energy were categories that didn't cross my mind as something to be aware of, strive for, uncover, shape or balance. The goal for me was getting exposure and access to better or more prestigious work options, so that I could ultimately support myself, and raise a family. I wanted to live my self-sufficient, happily-ever-after with a working spouse. While I knew it was the very institutions I was looking to access which perpetuated inequality, I was on a mission to level the playing field by inserting my qualified face into those circles.

Simultaneously, I was thinking about the meanings of motherhood, wife, and family in the context of what I thought defined womanhood. If I was concerned with working and being competitive and successful, what kind of mother would I have time to be? What would it be like to be married to me and what kind of wife would I be? I knew for certain I was raised by a professionally successful, divorced mother who had two daughters, accomplished an advanced degree while I was in junior high school, and worked two jobs across two NYC boroughs and daily work shifts. There was no doubt that hard work and sacrifice were rules in my unwritten manual of what it means to be a woman. I knew what a father's love felt like, and what a mother's love and support looked like, but I didn't know firsthand what a wife did, or what a marriage looked like. Achieving motherhood in my current status as a single woman was a bit of an anomaly to me. *Was it possible?* In college, what I thought was true was I needed to be married in order to start a family. But that just didn't feel right.

Societal and familial indoctrination told me womanhood status was achieved through marriage and/or motherhood. Growing up I was often told by my mother, aunts, and older cousins that I wouldn't understand what it meant to be grown, or how difficult it was to be a mother, until one day when I had children of my own. I carried that foreshadowing with me for years after college graduation and through law school.

In addition to that proclamation, my tangible reality was invaded by consistent, physical discomfort from fibroids to remind me I was working against Mother Nature and my window of fertility would not stay open on my timetable. My proverbial biological clock was ticking, and I wasn't ready to start a family. Positioning myself for the realities of motherhood seemed difficult, illogical, irresponsible, and expensive.

Post law school, I started socially identifying with groups I believed were appropriate for my personal development. They included empowerment groups, professional organizations, cultural, and other support and uplift groups. However, it often seemed to me they attracted women who needed a break from their husbands and families, rather than those who were husband hunting or seeking clarity.

About five years apart, between my late twenties and early thirties, I had a couple fibroid surgeries to remove the invaders which kept coming back like rude house guests. After a few years of taking up silent residence in my body, the first set of tumors would make their presence known by pressing on my bladder. "False alarm" urges to urinate were constant. The next set prolonged my menstrual cycle, and further disrupted my hormonal health by causing spotting in between cycles. They manifested as the aggressive results of the self-inflicted and socially constructed mental and emotional stress I had been experiencing professionally and personally. They were fueled by my repressed feelings of inadequacy. While I was insecure about the slow rate at which I made professional and personal progress, their physical presence and energy were thriving and multiplying. They were overwhelming me, and needed to be purged again. I scheduled another surgery in my late thirties.

It wasn't until the day I was in the doctor's office discussing my pre-surgery scans, I realized these fibroid tumors were more serious than before. There were more of them, and they were pervasive. In the battle of me against my fibroids, they were winning. This time there were so many, the sonogram couldn't see my fallopian tubes clearly. Remembering images from high school science classes helped me grasp the severity of that fact. Discussing the repercussions of the fibroid invasion with my doctor opened a whole new world of considerations about motherhood.

My options were:

Option 1) Have the surgery, and if everything was successful, and if I got pregnant at a later date, I'd deliver my baby via c-section as a vaginal delivery would likely harm me and my baby because of scar tissue and stress on my uterus from prior surgeries.

Option 2) Postpone the surgery until I tried to preserve some of my eggs, in case the surgery didn't go well.

No slight decision and no guarantees either way. I chose Option 2. With the start of my new exclusively-work-from-home job, I'd be allowed some privacy without having to commute to an office or take much time off for healing.

Quickly I had to figure out whether I wanted to just retrieve and preserve eggs, or preserve embryos. In just a few short weeks, my focus shifted from scheduling my surgery, to searching for a fertility specialist to conduct the procedures for retrieving, preserving, and fertilizing my eggs. Robotically and methodically, I got a referral and kept a level head because my future was at stake. My legacy was on the line. What would be left of the Sackeys when I was gone?

I reassessed how I wanted to start my family. Did I want to be in a loving relationship with a spouse who also wanted to raise children? Of course! But I wasn't in a relationship, and it didn't resonate with me that I had to wait until I found "the one" to either have permission, or be granted the privilege of motherhood.

The weight of my situation added more ingredients to the pot, self-blame and guilt. The simmer of shame and anger rose to a boil as I thought to myself, how had I let so much time slip away from me? How had I so narrowly focused on only external parts of myself and not my *whole* self?

From Disappointment to Surprise: Part II

I always knew I'd be a mommy in my own right. I had too much to share with and learn from a little one. And so I did it. I started the in vitro fertilization process for my fortieth birthday. On my celebratory yoga retreat, I traveled with my ovarian stimulation medications and injected myself at the same times every day, alternating which side of my body I pricked as I began to feel like tenderized meat. I am not squeamish. I did not have trouble with the needles. I had my eyes on the prize: get as many eggs as possible! No pain, no gain!

Shortly after returning home from my trip, multiple eggs were retrieved, more than half a dozen. My eggs were fertilized and most were able to be preserved. Then the embryos were tested for genetic abnormalities. While I waited for the results, I busied myself with work at my new job, only to find out after a few weeks that for multiple reasons, none of the embryos were viable. Therefore, none would be transferred. The experts assured me I would have had multiple miscarriages had the embryos been implanted. The news was delivered over the phone while I was working from home, and I didn't have time to process the impact. More devastatingly, I didn't have anyone to process it with. No one else was personally invested or affected by the outcome but me. Those who I did share the news with told me to take one step at a time and not get too far ahead of myself, or too deep into my feelings.

I was sliding backwards into low vibration, negative feelings: *I should have known it would turn out that way; I should have done it sooner, and not waited until a medical reason presented itself.*

My 401K and savings were depleted because the medical tests, prescriptions, doctor visits, and most of the procedures were not covered by insurance. I couldn't afford round two. But I found comfort in the fact I had tried, and would never have to wonder whether I should have tried the IVF process.

I'd told a few of my friends I was doing IVF, so I had to follow up and tell them the process was unsuccessful, there wouldn't be a baby shower to plan, and I was having another surgery. I sped through the conversations reciting facts and not getting caught up in the details. My third and last fibroid surgery successfully evicted fifty-five fibroids. There were no complications; but I knew they'd grow back. The stress wasn't gone.

I was not ready to let go of becoming pregnant, but my body needed time to heal from fifty-five new scars and adhesions before I considered any other options to motherhood through pregnancy. What now? This part of my life's linear plan was not on my mental notes list. When I heard, "You should (become a) foster (parent)" or "Can't you just foster or adopt?" from my married friends, or those who had experienced pregnancy, and given birth to their children, I was offended. Hadn't I attended their weddings, baby showers, children's birthday parties? Now they were suggesting I consider an option none of them had done.

A week or two later, realizing my friends had made good points and presented me with new information I hadn't considered, I looked at adoption. I tried to define it. Typically, the outcome of adoption is permanent, unlike fostering. What I already knew about it was what I'd seen in the media with celebrities' internationally adopted children, or transracially adopted peers I knew when I was school age. There were also TV shows and horrible news stories of children being stolen without their birth mother or biological family's knowledge and secretly sold to other families. These stories were often recounted whenever I tried to casually inquire about people's opinions on the topic. I also knew stories about intrafamilial adoptions in which children had officially or unofficially been raised by members of their extended families.

But what would adoption look like for me? What were my options? Where did I fit into all these scenarios? I hadn't researched this. I was spiraling. I switched gears and asked questions of a few personal friends—one who used to work for an adoption agency, a couple others who had a close friend or family member who'd adopted at least one child. None of these valued members of my life knew each other personally, but the name of a specific private adoption agency came up repeatedly. I took this as a sign. I checked out their website and clicked the link to express my interest.

Informational webinars, a personal statement, references, medical history questionnaires, financial portfolio inquiries, home study visits, CPR classes, a background check and fingerprints, adoption education classes, child development seminars, pictures for my profile….Fulfilling all these prerequisites helped the time pass from showing interest and signing up in early 2017, to becoming eligible to adopt later that year. I was relieved there was a support system in place and mapped out steps for me to follow. I was tired of researching, thinking and planning alone. But nothing would speed up the subsequent waiting time until a match was made in the summer of 2019.

I had never before felt so judged and scrutinized, and admittedly

I resented it. My insecurities rose to the surface again, but I had dug in my heels, put in the work, and was undeterred. With a pregnancy, you can anticipate a due date. With adoption, you don't know when it will happen, but there was no doubt in my heart I would become a mother.

> My insecurities rose to the surface again, but I had dug in my heels, put in the work, and was undeterred.

Getting Grounded and Heading Into My Right of Passage

I could be patient. Understanding the weight of the responsibility of being a mother, the priority of the child's best interest, the consideration for the well-being of the birth mother and her choice to love her child from afar, and the legal obligations of the agency, I quickly got over myself. However, I couldn't help but feel an adoption-like process should be required of *all* parents-to-be. You are vetted in ways no biological parent ever is, made to think about questions not usually considered before pregnancy, and anticipate and prepare for a plethora of what-if scenarios in life. For example, many of the parents I knew didn't know infant CPR.

The waiting time was actually a blessing. I had time to get myself rooted in a sense of self-identity that would support my personal development, my physical well-being, my sanity, a sacred union when I was ready to receive it, and my ability to facilitate a child's growth—except, maybe not in that order. The talk therapy continued, but there was a different type of healing I needed. Yoga had started to help six years earlier, but that was just the beginning of the spiritual path I was opening up to.

At this time in my life, on the other side of forty, I often recalled lyrics to songs from the acapella group, *Sweet Honey In The Rock*. More mature and contemplative than I was when they were first imprinted upon me during a Carnegie Hall concert at the age of twelve, those lyrics, adapted from the original poem by Khalil Gibran, *On Children* from *The Prophet*, never left my mind:

Your children are not your children / They are the sons and the daughters of Life's longing for itself / They come through you / but they are not from you / And though they are with you / they belong not to you.

I had always focused on, "they come *through* you, but they are not from you." I kept wondering how to bring a child through me. I understood that we as parents are vessels, but not creators. I understood that there was a spiritual component to the cycle of life that included being allowed to plant a seed, grow a human, and feed that human from the milk of your body. But I had been approaching it from the physical realm, and had been glossing over the previous lyric, "They are the sons and daughters of Life's longing for itself."

Now, as more pieces of the picture came into focus, I extracted the preceding thought in the song. Both literally and figuratively, this was the most pivotal component in determining when *my* child would come *through*; come into spiritual being.

It was when Life longed to live.

There had always been a feeling that something was pulling me from the other side of the parental relationship. Motherhood resonated with me more than wifehood. I wasn't just ready to be a mother, there was a soul ready to be my child, and he was reaching out for me. He was going to make sure he got here because he longed to be here, with me. He was waiting for me to catch up, because I still had my doubts and hesitations. I tried to presuppose what a birth mother would think of me: *Could I really be enough of a parent as a single mother?* I thought, *What chance did I have to compete with two-parent households?* Bankruptcy allowed me to alleviate most of my debt, except my student loans. *What would possess me to take on adoption expenses and raising a child on one household income?* The answer was I knew I could do it. I knew I was supposed to *do* it. I knew I was supposed to *be* it. A mother. His mother. I knew nothing would stop me. I told my brain to shut up and let it happen. I even had a dream where I saw myself feeding my baby.

I stopped selling myself short. If I could think it and believe it, then it was possible, even if I didn't know how or when to make it so. At no point did I think I wouldn't get matched with a birth family; I just didn't know how long it would take. I could live with that because I had work to do in the meantime.

The Spiritual Awakening

We never know. The adoption waiting period can take months or years. My social worker warned me about preparing before knowing. It could be a boy or a girl—keep clothing gender neutral. Don't buy a crib yet—it may be empty for a while. I did start thinking about boy and girl names, but felt like I wouldn't be able to settle on one until I met him or her. I realized I had surrendered. That surrendering meant letting go, not giving up. Keep it moving; because time is *not* linear. My timeline was not the only one at work. I enjoyed myself by continuing to live my life, and I just stopped thinking about it. I went on vacations, learned to play golf, moved to a larger apartment, started a new job, and even started a new relationship.

While I waited, I also decided to give myself the gift of a spiritual, healing course. The experience was offered by Queen Afua, a renowned author, Kemetic priestess, mentor, yoga teacher, herbalist, holistic health expert, and a mother. The course text was her book entitled, *Sacred Woman: A Guide to Healing The Feminine Body, Mind, and Spirit.* This self-discovery course is what finally ushered in my rite of passage to womanhood! It gave me the gift of vision and self-actualization through meditation, changes in my diet, daily prayers, and study of ancient Kemetic deities and the spirits of my ancestors.

Previously, I hadn't been able to see or articulate the breakdown in my femininity from a spiritual point of view. First came the confirmation I was already a complete woman, a whole person. Then came the realization that what I needed was to formally redefine motherhood. To redefine "coming through." To redefine womb and birth from a divinely feminine point of view, rather than from the masculine perspective I'd been steeped in.

Once more, I recalled a song from *Sweet Honey In The Rock*. The lyrics were adapted from a poem by Birago Diop called, *Breaths*:

Listen more often to things than to beings / 'Tis the ancestor's word
/ When the fire's voice is heard / 'Tis the ancestor's word /
In the voice of the waters / Ah-ahh, wshh, ahh-wshh
/ Those who have died have never, never left / ....

By recognizing the ancestors and "listening to things," I better understood what "Life's longing" meant. The course helped me shift and see motherhood wasn't about using my physical womb, but about acknowledging I had the ability to build and create a family structure. Also, I embraced and settled on the fact I was not in competition with any other parents-to-be, because we were not meant to parent the same child.

The thread of balance marked this awakening stage of my life. The leveling out of masculine and feminine energies. I had been trained to be outwardly focused on living my life by seeking labels and membership in categories based upon what I did. I had allowed myself to be impacted upon, identified, and devastated by scenarios keyed to activities performed, rather than who I was. My academic training and legal career sent my energy outward using masculine markers, traits, and values to pursue success. Seeking external validation and power had overtaken my inner feminine authority, insight, sense of what I could control, and my overall vibe. Shifting my focus inward was life-changing. The life balancing process had started years earlier with a new job which inadvertently created a better environment for healing after attempting IVF. Another new job started a year before I got The Call to become a mother, and allowed for a separation and balance between work and home life. I was ready to let go of trying to gather things and labels I gave power and meaning to, without which I deemed myself unsuccessful. Instead, I claimed my inner desires and listened to the whispers that came out of my renewed consciousness, and from my ancestors.

Lessons Learned

I now define femininity as an energy or a frequency. Frequencies are transmitted; they can be high or low; they can be interrupted or dispersed. The higher the frequency, the higher the energy. When my frequency was interfered with, clarity turned to noisy static. The noise clouded my vision, and disrupted my thought processes, perception of the world, and my own life choices. The outward focus of my energy caused a transfer of my frequency to no one in particular. Therefore, who could resonate with it and reflect it back to me? I was honed in on seeking independence rather than interconnectedness. Without knowing how to describe what I was experiencing, and what I was living without, I resented what it looked like and how it felt.

I took the Sacred Woman course after the IVF process. This course taught me not only to open my proverbial third eye, but to open my heart, as well as open my inner ear. There were pathways and gateways that led to higher states of awareness which my classmates and I walked through as we integrated spiritual principles and affirmations into our daily lives. Peeling back the layers, I uncovered how I'd used my masculine mind to the detriment of my feminine heart. I realized we women often push feelings aside and allow others to color our perception of the choices we should make when it comes to career, family, and self-identity.

Through the rite of passage, I rose from the level of woman, to that of a Sacred Woman. I defined myself as such and was now firmly grounded in that inner truth. I had defined motherhood as based upon the presence of another, in the context of being a wife, or being pregnant and physically birthing, but I realized I was a spiritual woman and mother to many. My first child had been my inner child. I wanted more children, so I looked further and cast my net wider.

I surrendered to my divine femininity because I had the power to manifest.

Other gateways we worked with delved into our intuition and creative

My first child had been my inner child.

vision. It was here I learned a womb is where creativity is grown and nurtured, until ideas are ready to be 'birthed'. With the tools I was given,

I was able to start healing past wounds of self-doubt, and learn how to sit in silence and summon my inner voice and inner knowing. She is certain and unwavering, committed to the task at hand, and softer than I thought she would be, grounded in her strength, not limited by it. Once I overcame my negative self-talk that the outside world had turned into a constant inner critic, and a voice of caution, I was able to realize my true inner voice would never steer me wrong or betray my heart. This was my intuition.

Graduation day from the course was called our Ascension. I chose the Goddess Ast as a representation of my growth into a multi-faceted, mature, grown woman. She is an Ascended Master, known as the Great Mother and represents sacred unions, completely redefining the context of marriage for me. Ast is also known as the Goddess of Sovereignty, the Queen of the Ancestors, and the Goddess of many titles. There was a spiritual union first between me and my Creator, then me and my Self, and finally me and my Family. It wasn't until I had ascended during graduation and walked *through* my chosen gateway that I was ready to align with my child who was on the other side. I felt the calling because it was already done. I had manifested my family. As I ascended, the parallel timeline of *Life's longing for itself* was coming through, because less than a year later my son was born.

My Victory

I received a couple calls from the adoption agency asking for permission to submit my personal statement and profile to a birth family. Then there was a long lag of time. After an extended Fourth of July weekend getaway in New Jersey, I was contacted by my social worker. She left me a voicemail saying she'd like to speak with me about a birth mother who was interested in my profile! I was in transit and had missed the call. I checked my email and there was a message there too! I got off the train before my destination to return her call. In just that short amount of time the message she had left turned into, "She (the birth mother) chose you and she wants to meet you!" The match notification was on Monday, the in-person match meeting was on Tuesday. The following Monday I held my perfectly beautiful two-and-a-half-week-old son in my arms!

I could not have been *grounded*—as in centered—if I'd remained grounded—as in tethered and unable to move. My lifetime of conditioning and programming consciously and unconsciously affected the choices I made, and the emphasis I placed on what was important in life. Some choices were instinctual, some were made after careful deliberation. When deliberating, I had to be aware of the limiting beliefs I considered. I didn't go into this process knowing how to overcome those beliefs, but I was at least aware they existed. I asked for what I thought I wanted, but that was initially based upon what I had been told I *should* want, and upon where I thought I was supposed to go—marriage by a certain age, children by a certain age, completion of education by a certain age, and a substantial salary by a certain age.

After I had passed a maturity threshold, I again asked for what I wanted, but left room for more, for what I didn't even know I wanted. I didn't just ask for a child, because I didn't know how to define him; that would have been limiting. I asked for a situation, a circumstance, a feeling. I wanted to have the parent/child relationship and learn from this person I was supposed to teach. The soul I was supposed to guide. Here, I surrendered and allowed the power to manifest to come through me as I watched it happen.

I don't have it all figured out. I am still learning, and some days are better than others. What I do know, however, is we are here to learn until our last day, there is no cut-off point where we know everything. Our learning curve is infinite, not based upon what schools we went to, or how much we earn. I am still working on myself. I surrender in some way every day, and I am not "there" yet. I haven't arrived. I am happy about this because I choose to be happy. No one else can do that for me. The Journey continues.

Chotsani (CJ) Sackey

Chotsani (CJ) Sackey, daughter of Crucian and African-American parentage, is herself a mother, author, attorney, and aspiring entrepreneur. Those titles assign her to multitask as a proactive manager, information gatherer, problem solver, and collaborator.

Chotsani's commitment to fairness and justice was sparked at Wesleyan University. She subsequently earned her law degree from Rutgers University and has worked for several New York City law firms and organizations during her career. Currently, as an in-house government attorney, she is responsible for managing discovery requests, and ensuring compliance with document retention requirements. Twenty years after earning her law degree, this Human Design Reflector is reinventing herself to continue to be of service while embracing her joy.

Chotsani is the proud mother of a 3-year-old ray of Sonshine. She is committed to being the spiritual guide he chose her to be for him.

She regularly takes advantage of her proximity to the New York Botanical Garden in the Bronx to get grounded and centered in nature. She considers herself a yogini, and in her almost non-existent spare time, enjoys coloring mandalas. Chotsani also loves to *accidentally* fall soundly asleep during meditation, and strives to keep her house plants alive.

CONNECT WITH CHOTSANI

 solo.to/cjsackey

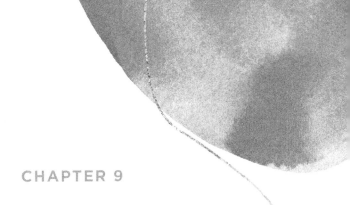

CHAPTER 9

In Order to Be the Light, One Must First Feel All of the Darkness

By Wiaam Yasin

> TRIGGER WARNING: This chapter includes information that may be difficult to read and/or digest such as sexual abuse, rape, and suicidal ideation. I strongly encourage you to care for your own well-being while reading.

"What did you just say?" unsure if I really heard those verbal weapons come out of my husband's mouth. "Call the police because I'm going to kill you," he repeated, raging with such violent and uncontrolled anger. Yup, he said it again. It wasn't in my head. I was frozen, shocked, and completely disassociated from what I had just experienced.

Four years of accumulated patterns, unchanged behavior, and cycles of abuse. That was it. I packed my bags with conviction in my heart and texted my sister to pick up my two-month-old son and me.

The text exchange went something like this:

Me: "Can you pick me up?"

Her: "Right now?"

Me: "Yes"

Her: "Be there in 15".

That was the last time I ever laid foot in that apartment.

We arrived at my parent's house safely that evening, and I slept well that night, knowing that my son and I were safe. My body may have also been preparing me for the countless sleepless nights to come.

By the time my marriage had ended, my mind, body, and spirit were completely wounded, broken, and lost. My physical body was spazzing out, literally. The trapped emotions manifested physically as body tremors, shaking, and trembling. I felt that I had no control over what was happening to me, which was one of my worst nightmares; not being in control.

I revealed to my family in the days and weeks to follow what triggered my homecoming, and this is when all of the

> I felt that I had no control over what was happening to me, which was one of my worst nightmares; not being in control.

trauma began to unleash as I finally verbalized what I was experiencing throughout the four years of my marriage, a mental prison. It was as if my lips had been taped shut, and I was finally able to speak the truth when I was no longer under his control.

When I finally sat down to write and process the emotions from the series of events that had just occurred, I began to feel flooded. I felt I couldn't breathe. The shaking intensified.

"Mama! I'm dying! Call Baba and Maab right now, I'm dying!"

I ran over to my mother who was in the room with me, as I'm in complete and utter terror. My son was asleep throughout this. My dad and sister, Maab, went back to my apartment to clear out my belongings at the time, without me, as I did not feel safe laying foot in the space where my life was threatened. My mom called them to come home, and they came to tend to me immediately.

It was heavy and terrifying to confront everything I had subconsciously avoided for this very reason. This is what death must feel like, I thought to myself, with a part of me believing that death was this horrible and painful punishment from God, disconnected at the time from who my Creator really is. Another part of me believed that I experienced the injustices in my marriage just so I could pass away and be compensated for it in the Heavens, a belief I carried that "you struggle in this life so you can be celebrated in the Next." I had several conflicting beliefs come alive for me at once.

"Wiaam, give me a hug, I think you're having a panic attack," my mother said to me.

This wasn't a panic attack. I'd had panic attacks before. I was having a nervous breakdown.

Panic attacks usually decrease in intensity after ten minutes or so. A nervous breakdown can last over a period of time and temporarily restricts a person's ability to function in multiple areas of their life.

I resisted my mother's hug, feeling terrified as hell, "No, Mama, I'm dying, Mama, I'm dying!" I yelled and cried hysterically. No one believed me and that was making me feel even more insane.

I had her call my youngest sister, Matab, who drove two hours from where she was to come and be with me in my trauma. She brought her weighted blanket to lend me. It aided me in the anxious nights to follow. My brother, Muhammad, who lives out of state, was out when I called him and received a call from me telling him "I'm dying!" He immediately left where he was to be on the phone with me for the next hour as he coached me through my breakdown on speakerphone, along with the family members and loved ones in the room with me.

I called three close friends, Aqsa, Razan, and Riham, who stopped everything they were doing to support me. They walked upstairs to the room where I was staying at my parent's house, with their masks on, finding me wailing in a completely hysterical state, all while breastfeeding my son, hearing me say what I truly believed to be my last words. This was all taking place during the height of the Black Lives Matter movement and the COVID-19 pandemic. I hadn't seen these friends in a significantly long time, and when they did see me, here I was, completely undone.

I remember everyone in the room looking at me with helplessness and heartbreak as I broke down. My aunt, Ibtisam, who passed away one year later from Stage IV cancer, was also present. I remember her pacing back and forth in the room, looking visibly anxious and unsettled, yet still trying to keep her composure to support me. I was surrounded by love.

Although I was supported entirely during this time externally, it did not take away from this intense fear, hopelessness, and despair I was feeling internally. I realize now that I had manifested my deepest fear of abandonment. All of those years, I thought to myself, if I had continued to prove my worth to him, I would be respected. I would be seen, heard, and loved—seeking the love from him that was within me all along.

It's funny how that works, isn't it? The love we seek outside often comes from a void within. What's the wound? Where does it come from? What beliefs have brought forth this experience? What feels missing, and how can I give that to myself? This has been my journey of awakening.

My father anxiously called our local Imam who is also our dear family friend, Imam Muhammad Magid, in the midst of this nervous breakdown I was having. My dad and Imam Magid's support for me were unwavering. It was comforting to know that there were men in my life who cared and were protective of me, my brother included.

Imam Magid quickly and swiftly ensured the religious initiation of my divorce would be completed immediately, reassuring me that my former husband's behavior was unacceptable and would not be tolerated in our community. I was relieved by his validation and support.

"Imam Magid, I'm dying. Listen to me. I am dying! Tell the community to make dua (prayers, supplications) for me. Don't believe anything he tells you, he is a liar! Imam Magid, he is a liar!" I cried, "Imam Magid, please, tell the community to pray for me! I'm dying, I'm dying!"

He attempted to reassure me that I was having a panic attack and that everything was going to be okay, but at the time, nothing could get through to this visceral experience I was having. No one could comfort me.

During this breakdown, I was also instructing my sister on tasks that need to get done on my behalf before or once I leave earth, "Take him off of my financial accounts. List Amin as my beneficiary. You can read all of my journals—all of the proof is there! Listen to your intuition, because that is Allah speaking to you!" I cried.

The internalized injustices exploded out of me all at once. "Black lives matter. Black lives matter. Black lives matter!" I continued to wail as I cried through the words of my heart, feeling the anger, pain, and injustices of George Floyd's death, while also remembering the infuriating arguments I had with my former husband, who would defend the police, although black himself.

"They do," my sister affirmed.

I cried hysterically to my sweet baby boy while telling him he is going to be okay without his mother, and that I love him. I will never forget how he looked into my eyes as I breastfed him, on one hand, unaware of what was happening yet on another, very much attuned to his mother's pain.

I asked my parents for forgiveness and told each of my family members and friends in the room that I loved them and to pray for me, and not to worry about me, because God is with the oppressed, so I was going to Heaven. I put on a dress that I believed I would be passing away in.

I was ready to leave this Earth.

This episode lasted about an hour. When it finally ended, I took some breaths, washed my hands, face, and feet as I performed *wudu*, (ablution, a washing ritual done for prayer in Islam) and prayed *salat al-Maghrib*, the Sunset prayer, one of the five Muslim daily prayers. I survived. The act of performing *wudu* felt healing in itself, as I released and washed off the energy from that episode.

Although I felt a temporary sense of relief after that purge, in the days and weeks following this ordeal, waking up to my reality was absolutely dreadful. I was severely depressed and suffered from Complex Post-Traumatic Stress Disorder (C-PTSD). I could barely eat, and I could not sleep. The breastmilk supply that I had worked so hard to produce slowly diminished as a result of the distress I was in until it eventually dried out.

Right before this breakdown, my former husband and I got on the phone for the last time to mutually agree to proceed with the divorce. He cried saying how he couldn't believe he was losing his family, and that he needed me. The guilt washed over me. This cycle was all too familiar.

Right when I started to feel this immense guilt, the Most High sent me another confirmation. I received an "accidental" voice note from my former husband, shortly after he just cried to me on the phone, talking to his friend about a woman's breasts that he saw walking down the street.

I can't forget what I heard. I felt nauseous and physically sick to my stomach. I did not recognize that person. The veil had been lifted, and the truth was being revealed.

Every day, or it felt like every hour, I would connect more dots, like how he suddenly decided he wanted to become a pilot after learning about my intense fear of flying. He made it seem as though this had been a career passion of his for a long time, so I supported him in this pursuit and visited flight schools with him.

Gag. He thrived off my pain. I could not believe it. The fear of flying developed after I got married. It threw me off guard one day as I was on a plane to Florida for a work trip, and the anxiety on that flight was unbearable. I told myself I would drive back home after that experience. I later learned that this fear of flying stemmed from feeling unsafe in my marriage, and a lack of control.

The same went for elevators. I couldn't be in them anymore, especially alone. I would take the stairs although I worked on the eighth floor of my work building at the time. It was good exercise, but that wasn't my intention. I couldn't risk getting stuck. These fears reflected my internal state of feeling trapped and living in paralyzing fear—being in an elevator and airplane reminded me of that.

Following these incidents, the realizations, and the nervous breakdown, I could not bear to be with myself. Someone in my family had to be with me at all times. I went to the bathroom with the door open. I had nightmares nearly every night for the next few weeks that my former husband, or another man, was out to murder me. I could not walk outside without looking over my shoulder. I did not feel safe existing.

I made sure the locks on the doors of our house were changed. I had loved ones look up shelters for me, in case I had to go into hiding. I remember crying to my therapist in one session telling her, "Michelle, if

I die as a result of this, it is not your fault." I genuinely believed that this man was going to kill me.

I remember listening to Tupac's "Keep Ya Head Up," as that was one of my go-to songs when I needed some upliftment. I felt like he was speaking directly to me as he acknowledged the single mothers who were mistreated by their men and the injustices of misogyny. I find every line of that song to be powerful, but this part, in particular, truly moves my spirit:

You know what makes me unhappy?
When brothers make babies and leave a young mother to be a pappy.

And since we all came from a woman,
got our name from a woman,
and our game from a woman,
I wonder why we take from our women?
Why we rape our women?
Do we hate our women?

I think it's time to kill for our women.
Time to heal our women.
Be real to our women.

And if we don't, we'll have a race of babies,
that will hate the ladies,
that make the babies.

And since a man can't make one,
He has no right to tell a woman when and where to create one.

So will the real men get up?
I know you're fed up ladies, but keep your head up.

I felt like the Divine was speaking to me through these words, every single time. Amin would even kick extra hard when I played that song during my pregnancy, as he jammed with me in my womb. That song grounded me, but at this particularly dark time in my life, when I listened and heard the part, "We ain't meant to survive, 'cause it's a setup," I felt my heart sink into my stomach. I remembered how Tupac was murdered. It was another reminder that the world isn't safe. I began to spiral. The body tremors surfaced again, along with the uncontrollable shaking. I'm dying, I'm dying, I'm dying. I had a panic attack. Everything triggered me, even my favorite song.

While right in the thick of it, I received news that a childhood friend, Lojain Elsadig, had suddenly passed away in a car accident. She was interviewing at my job at the time and we were just talking about how excited we were to soon be working together. She also mailed me a gift the week before for the birth of my son and shared with me her intention of throwing me a baby shower in her home after the pandemic. Her presence in my life was like this illuminating light that I still feel within me today. Her passing intensified the darkness and fear of death that I was already experiencing at the time. I could not wrap my mind around my current reality. I felt like the world was crashing down on me.

Through this series of devastating events, I started to question: What is the purpose? Heartache, after heartache, after heartache—why? What about this "concept" of joy? What is that? Is it real? Is it possible for one to experience it in this lifetime? If so, is it available for me?

Little did I know the Most High was working through me, triggering these experiences for me to ask these very questions, and awaken to the truth that I had been so severely disconnected from.

While married, I slept alone nearly every night, believing that my husband was out working, not knowing at the time that he was out indulging in addictions, infidelity, and a life that I never in my wildest dreams would have believed he was capable of living. I believed his excuses for coming home late. I trusted him, more than I trusted myself, and perhaps that was the culprit.

Something didn't feel right, but I was extremely confused. When the suspicions would arise, he knew exactly what to say to convince me otherwise of what I was feeling. On one hand, I felt like he was a good man. He was sweet and caring towards me, when he wanted to be, and especially kind and sweet to everyone else. He even regularly expressed his gratitude for me. He prayed five times a day. He would kiss my father on his head when he greeted him. He helped around the house. He played the part so incredibly well, yet something still felt off.

It felt like a never-ending internal and external conflict. With every red flag, every episode of rage, followed by a remorseful apology, followed by reconciliation and a good time, followed by some more manipulation, which caused me to question him, causing another episode of rage, and then back to the same episode. I was extremely confused as I went through these cycles, except my heart always knew. My heart knew I wasn't deserving of what I was enduring, though I hadn't learned yet that trusting how I feel is enough.

The way this man presented himself to be, versus who he actually was, in itself was a huge part of the illusion. I feared that no one would believe me if I told them what I was experiencing. He wore his mask so well, and so did I, pretending everything was fine, doing exactly what cultural norms taught us.

My son and I often watched and listened to the song "Let it Go" from the movie *Frozen*. The way he sings it makes my heart melt. I remember the lyrics hitting home as we sang, *"Don't let them in, don't let them see. Be the good girl you always have to be. Conceal, don't feel, don't let them know. Well, now they know. Let it go, let it go…"*

What made me feel more disconnected from my Source and Creator, was that someone could pray five times a day without fail and severely mistreat his wife. It blew my mind. I knew that wasn't what my faith taught, but the hypocrisy tainted me. There are countless references in both the *hadith* (narrations of the Prophet, peace be upon him) and the Qur'an that strongly condemn the injustices I was experiencing, yet my former husband manipulated religion to fit his agenda, and it completely distorted my spiritual reality.

He told me that it was my religious duty to "give him sex" on-demand at any time, and if I didn't, God would be angry with me, and the angels would curse me. What is worse about this, is that at the time, I actually believed it. And yes, he used the words, "give him sex," as if sex is not a mutually beneficial exchange and a give-and-take encounter. He would regularly tell me that if I didn't fulfill his need for sex, all the time, he would find it elsewhere, and he was serious.

I wish I had the words to accurately express the impact that this had on me.

I was internally in shambles. I felt like everything I was experiencing was my fault, especially considering that I had discovered a childhood sexual trauma that I experienced after attempting to lose my virginity.

I still forced myself to have sex, despite the psychological impact it had on me. I would cringe with my hands over my face, in tears, while getting raped during the entirety of my marriage, unable to name it what it was at the time. I felt absolutely worthless. There was no way in hell I could tell anyone this. I felt trapped, and that showed up in interesting ways, such as my fear of flying and elevators.

I hated myself for what I was experiencing. I struggled with suicidal ideation. It felt like the only escape. I remember when a childhood friend that I was especially close to in elementary and middle school, Ariana Ahmed, passed away due to suicide, feeling such an intensity of complicated grief, as it evoked the dark and suicidal thoughts that I was experiencing within myself. The depression worsened.

I was manipulated into believing I was the problem, so I sought therapy for it. So there I was, in therapy, working on this issue I have of "not enjoying sex" with my spouse, believing that it stemmed from my own childhood trauma, meanwhile, I was getting raped, and unable to express it that way. Imagine getting sexually abused while trying to heal from sexual abuse. That was my reality. He used my wounds against me. This wasn't about my childhood trauma, which I had actively been working on healing, this was about manipulation and exertion of control and power. He was also adamantly against me going to therapy. It makes sense now. As long as I was unhealed, he could control me. He feared the person he knew I would become.

> He feared the person he knew I would become.

After intercourse, or allow me to simply name it what it was, **rape**, I would have nightmares. I remember waking up in a panic, crying and begging him to please, please stop. When I would tell him about these nightmares, in an effort to have him simply respect my needs, he would play victim, and ask, "Are you calling me your nightmare?" with a look of sadness in his eyes. I then felt guilty, and angry for even sharing this with him. How dare he play victim after raping his wife? I was at a loss. As I recount this, I feel called to emphasize that marital rape is real, and it deeply saddens me that I feel called to emphasize that.

I desperately needed to escape this torture I was experiencing. *How do women survive these types of circumstances? How do they come out on the other side?* I wondered. I remember watching an interview between Oprah and Gabrielle Union during those days, two magnificently inspirational survivors who transmuted their own trauma into purpose. Gabrielle Union's words truly struck a chord in me, when I heard her say, she felt like she was "screaming into a hurricane and no one could hear her." I felt this on such a deep, visceral level. She put into words exactly what I was feeling and could not articulate at the time.

I would often spend my nights alone journaling, having friends over, or connecting with a loved one on the phone, creating a life for myself to escape the darkness that I was experiencing. I also distracted myself by focusing on other people's needs. It was a great escape from my own reality.

These were some of the thoughts I was having at the time:

Just keep it in, Wiaam. Don't let them in. It's not safe. Stay distracted, it numbs the pain. Keep forward-thinking. If you pretend to be happy, perhaps you will be. Don't burden others with what you are going through. You can handle this. Marriage is hard. You can overcome this. It won't be like this forever. All couples go through struggles. You know the real him, Wiaam. He loves you. He is just struggling right now. He needs you. This will pass. He left everything behind to be with you. You can't just leave him. You can tolerate this, Wiaam. Keep swallowing the pain and hurt, it will go away. Things will get better, the voices told me.

I believed it was disloyal to share what goes on in my marriage outside of it, especially something as personal and intimate as sex. I believed that a "good Muslim girl" does not speak of such things. That was also part of the manipulation, this idea he planted of "what goes on between us stays between us."

But, what if I had it all wrong? What if being a "good Muslim girl" meant living in alignment with the truth of who you are?

What if being a "good Muslim girl" meant speaking the truth, regardless of how difficult it was? What if being a "good Muslim girl" meant trusting your heart? What if that is what truly pleased Allah? Hmm…I think I was onto something.

What if being a "good Muslim girl" meant speaking the truth, regardless of how difficult it was?

Voices from my higher self told me:

Wiaam, you do not deserve this treatment. You do not deserve this pain. You do not deserve to be living in a constant state of fear and suffering. There is more to life than this. Wiaam, this is not love.

Because I was aware of his hurt, and that hurt people hurt people, I felt inclined to stay, to heal him, to be with him in his pain. The guilt of leaving someone who I believed I loved and was hurting so much inside, ate at me. I felt this deep loyalty to him as his wife, this obligation to stay by my spouse's side through thick and thin.

I believed that as long as I healed, our marriage would work, because I was the problem, as was implied. I feared others judging him, as they wouldn't understand him the way I did. I also feared others judging me, for being in the relationship. A part of me fell for his manipulative tactics, and another part of me was deeply afraid of him. I was very much afraid of what he was capable of. I experienced enough fear to hinder me from exposing him, all while propelling me to leave when enough was enough.

All of the signs were there, and the hard pill to swallow is that they had always been there, though I wasn't ready to acknowledge them yet. That would mean having to make a decision I was not ready to make, which is why leaving my marriage and finally ending this cycle was such a significant breakthrough for me. My soul had been preparing me for this.

As I sat with the friends who were with me the night of my nervous breakdown in September 2020, I remember telling them, "I have to write about this." I had this deep inner calling to come out with this story. It felt too surreal, bizarre, and insane not to share. How many other women have experienced this and need to hear that they are not alone?

I will never forget what my friend, Riham, said to me that night, "I can't wait to see what you become, Wiaam. I can't wait to see what you become." These words have stayed with me. It gave me hope knowing that others saw something in me, not only in my ability to heal but to become something as a result.

I remember having several vivid dreams the week leading up to the separation. In one dream, I recall crying out to my mother, *Mama I'm not okay, I'm not okay*, and my mother crying with me in my dream. She felt me, both in the dream and in 'real' life. My mother had instinctively been feeling like I was not okay, questioning my own well-being, feeling that I was suffering in my marriage, questioning my former husband's behaviors, and begging me to open up, yet I was defensive of him and our marriage, and partly still living in denial. I wasn't able to tell her she was right, mostly because I had not acknowledged that truth to myself yet. I remember her calling me thirty minutes after taking a positive pregnancy test, and asking "Wiaam, are you pregnant? I just have this feeling you're pregnant. Wiaam, you better not be hiding this from me..." There is something to be said about a mother's intuition.

The next day, I had another dream that I was with my sweet son, and one of my sisters and my dad were there. It was dark, and I was trying to call out for help but I could not speak. I could not verbally ask for the help and support that I so desperately needed. It felt terrifying. These dreams rattled me. My soul was onto something, and then the day came when I left.

"And the day came when the risk
to remain tight in a bud was more painful
than the risk it took to blossom."

– ANAIS NIN

I am grateful to my therapist, Michelle, who shared that quote with me. I can genuinely say that I did everything I could to make things work, and the problem may have been that I was single-handedly trying to save a marriage on my own. I was willing to do any and everything to feel worthy of his love and respect. It makes me cringe now. I am grateful for how far I've come.

Consistent therapy sessions from a few weeks after my wedding date until today, the journey of healing continues. Because I was staying with my parents post-separation, I was relieved of the financial burdens I carried in my marriage and was able to truly invest in myself for what felt like the first time in my life. The first healing modality that I invested in, after traditional therapy, was NARP, the Narcissistic Abuse Recovery Program. What was significant about this program in my personal healing and recovery was: 1. learning that I was not alone in what I was experiencing, 2. realizing that healing is possible, as others had overcome and rebuilt their entire lives after having faced similar experiences, and 3. expanding my mind and heart to a different methodology of healing, one that was outside of my comfort zone. They say to get to where you've never been, you have to do what you've never done. For me, this meant giving myself permission to get back into the sacred body that I had disconnected from since childhood. It was time to come home. Coming home required me to identify and feel the traumas stored in my body, and be with them with compassion and unconditional love. NARP taught me this.

"For a seed to achieve its greatest expression, it must come completely undone. The shell cracks, its insides come out and everything changes. To someone who doesn't understand growth, it would look like complete destruction."

– CYNTHIA OCCELLI

Michelle shared that one with me, too. I continue to feel seen by her. It is such an integral aspect of a therapeutic relationship, to be seen, a need that was unfulfilled prior to working with her.

I had to become completely undone to become whole again, and it got worse before it got better. The body tremors increased over time; at one point it felt like I was having an exorcism until they eventually subsided. The tremors still appear from time to time when I feel overworked and stressed, and I receive them as signals from my nervous system telling me to slow down and rest. Sometimes they surface while I meditate, and that tells me shifts are taking place, as stagnant energy is released.

When I first began NARP, as I listened to the energy-healing modules and felt into the traumas in my body, I faced a lot of resistance. My mind attempted to conceptualize what could only be felt within my sacred body. I had so many questions: Is this permissible in my faith? Am I being misguided? I was hearing God being referred to as Source for the first time, and that brought up fear and discomfort. My ego was trying to make sense of what could only be felt in order to be released. Source, Spirit, God, Allah, the Divine—it was all the same. I came to learn that resistance is normal when our paradigm is being challenged. I would continue to face it in various ways while on the journey of healing and self-discovery.

Slowly but surely, as I began to feel safer in my body, I began to feel safer in the world around me. The nightmares lessened until they went away. I felt more connected with the Divine and with those around me. I began to experience a true sense of inner peace. I learned that joy is, in fact, real and that it is, in fact, available to me. Joy is within me, and as long as I am tuned into the essence of who I am, I am tuned into joy. I felt my paradigm begin to shift.

Once I could function on my own again, another key element of my recovery and healing was going into solitude. It was absolutely necessary. I needed to be with myself for some deep introspection, in silence, and in stillness. Naturally, I was releasing the patterns that no longer serve me, such as people pleasing, which was an especially difficult one to break. For the first time in my life, I was prioritizing my own needs, and I am so grateful that I did.

In tandem with therapy and NARP, I invested in one-on-one spiritual coaching, mainly because of the crisis I was having in my faith. The healing spaces I was in at the time were amazing, and felt safe, especially because they were non-religious, and at the same time, I felt I needed to talk to someone who understood the depths of spiritual abuse and religious shame I was experiencing, from an Islamic perspective. Speaking with Brother Ihsan Alexander was such a sigh of relief. Not only did he validate and normalize what I was experiencing, but he also helped bridge the gap between the healing work I was involved in and what Islam truly teaches. They were aligned.

This was groundbreaking for me. He spoke of the power of the breath, and that the word "Allah" in itself is a breath. He explained that religion without spirituality is like a body without a soul, confirming for me what I intuitively knew. Spirituality is truly what cultivates faith. It continues to be my saving grace. The disconnection was dissipating, and I was coming into union with all that is.

I have since allowed myself to remain open and curious. I find that the deeper I delve into healing and pursue what feels nurturing to my soul, the more I am guided to the most fitting resources, healing spaces, and people. I remember receiving an email from Jolie Dawn with an invitation to join Creatrix Expressed to heal through writing and join a community of like-minded women, shortly after setting the intention.

Allah was answering the call of my soul. It was up to me to receive those signs and take the inspired steps to transmute the pain into healing, purpose, and service to humanity.

I took one step towards Him, and He came to me running. Oh, how He came to me running.

Wiaam Yasin

Wiaam Yasin is a Sudanese American Muslim, a dreamer, a healer, and a spiritual being in this third dimension. As her name means harmony in Arabic, she is dedicated to embodying peace, love, and harmony within herself and the world around her. She currently makes a living as a project management consultant and is expected to become a certified hypnotherapist by the Fall of 2022.

Wiaam is also a proud single mother of her two-year-old son, Amin, [pronounced "Uh-meen"] whom she often refers to as Mino [pronounced "Mee-no"] and her Reeses Pieces. Wiaam is committed to fulfilling her soul mission of utilizing her personal healing journey to help heal herself and others. She deeply enjoys spending time in nature and connecting with the Earth from which she came and will someday return.

CONNECT WITH WIAAM

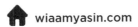 wiaamyasin.com

CHAPTER 10

Catching Fire

By Jen Miller

As I pulled around, straining my neck to check the carport-covered parking spot, the whole complex looked oddly foreign, and B's car was not there. My heart beat faster as I mentally replayed our last conversation like a tennis match. Had I missed something? His final comment whizzed past me as I analyzed it for context and meaning. While I had managed a response, it flew out of bounds, falling on deaf ears. B scored. The game is now fifteen, Love. His absence and lack of communication left me to guess where he was. He wouldn't have gone without saying goodbye, would he? It wasn't the first time he left me to cope with my runaway train of an imagination.

Still, I was growing concerned after his recent erratic behavior. Pushing that line of thinking away, I noticed the sidewalk was chipped and weathered, allowing little bits of moss and weeds to take hold. I regarded the plant's survival in a speck of dirt, avoiding the inevitable pedestrian demise or drought brought on by the relentless midday sun, as a minor miracle. But, disappointingly, I was in the minority. So I added to my mental checklist to pull out what the homeowners' association considered unsightly intruders. Recent temperatures were unseasonably high, triple digits with little breeze, and the moisture in the air was thick. I had heard B say, "If you don't like the weather in Texas, just wait a minute," which, I had learned, was a common expression in Texas.

As I turned the nearly worn-out brass doorknob, the crisp, cool, conditioned air and the faint aroma of vanilla greeted me. While the smell was familiar, something felt otherworldly like stepping to the edge of another dimension. Something was off. I scanned the rich mahogany wood-laminate floors, beige carpeting, and off-white, popcorn-textured ceiling. Despite a temperature of 95 degrees which felt like 105, a chill ran over me, causing my arm hairs to stand up. Glancing right, the kitchen, while in order, didn't seem welcoming as it usually had, and looking left, there was nothing out of place, but the room seemed more prominent and void of life. The living room should have held happy memories, and I let my eyes explore the space. Instead, it felt anything but happy. There was no laughter, color, warmth, or life. As I slowly lifted my gaze, still perplexed why my home felt so sterile, I saw it. As my eyes got to the loft at the top of the beige carpeted stairs, a small, familiar, out-of-place object sat defiantly, daring me to look closer. It seemed so innocuous sitting there, innocently trying to remind me of a long-ago moment in time, our first date. Reluctantly but determined, I stepped further inside, resigning myself to find out just what was happening.

That was the end of my life as I knew it.

I felt somehow smaller as I moved closer. I picked up the deliberately placed frame, glancing at the note, reading the words but not absorbing their meaning. My eyes were out of focus. I strained to see, but it was like looking through the lens of some warped viewfinder. My stomach lurched and flipped, and my balance failed; I caught myself with the railing. My body, usually so sure and confident in its motion, was no longer my own. As my limbs betrayed me, the photo tumbled down the stairs, cracking the glass. I saw his face, its expression mocking me.

My mind screamed, "Noooooo!" I then realized I was crying so hard I could not see, and my breathing had become ragged. I slumped to the carpeted steps, the fibers itchy on my skin. Wiping my eyes, it was then that I saw the note, simple but somehow so final. It simply read, "Always remember us this way." As those words traversed my troubled mind, it was like my spine refused its job and overwhelmed my senses. The room began to shift, and my lungs fought to work. What was happening? I was hyperventilating, panic oozing out of my pores as I broke into a cold, flop sweat. Everything about me seemed to grow smaller, weaker, and distant. My ears could not process sound; my stomach was forcing its way towards my tightening throat. Even the molecules of air were so much bigger than I was that I struggled to breathe. The room was spinning, and despite my best efforts to regain control, everything that was me shut down; my mind came to a screeching halt. Finally, as my eyes fluttered back into their sockets and eyelids squeezed shut, the room went dark and silent, and I collapsed unconscious.

⬤ ⬤ ⬤

I had no clue how much time had passed. Still, as I rubbed my eyes and brushed the carpet fibers from my cheek, I felt the bumpy impressions it left on my face and caught a glimpse of myself in the mirror hanging over the sofa. A tiny smile cracked fleetingly across my dry lips. Half of my face looked like a textured topographical map of Colorado, my chin boasting its best impression of a fourteen-thousand-foot mountain peak, and my nose covered in dried snot resembled a neighboring snow-capped summit. My cheek, pink and puffy, was wavy and textured like a Ruffle's Potato Chip. I was grateful that no one had seen me. I went to the primary bedroom; his suitcase was gone, the dresser half empty.

As the fleeting thoughts of salty chips and mountain peaks floated like a lazy river in my brain, the overwhelming cottonmouth got the best of me. I had to get something to drink. At that moment, I noticed the shadows from the fifteen-foot-high semi-circle window, with its broken shade and layer of unstoppable dust, were moving. Each passing degree of creeping shadow seemed to chase me into the kitchen. As I passed the round, glass-top table, I heaved a big sigh. I don't know if I had expected B to be standing there mixing his vodka concoction, but I felt disappointed. Shoulders slumped, I made my way to the refrigerator, trying to construct a likely scenario for why he wasn't home. He must have left for the rehabilitation facility early to avoid seeing me. No logical thoughts I had could make sense of the situation. It was apparent that there had been a strategic change in the plan. I thought about calling his mother but decided against it. His plan would undoubtedly have her involved as a complicit accomplice.

The tiny galley kitchen was just that, tiny. For two people to cook, timing, unspoken communication, intuitive abilities, and a cooperative nature would be required. Our personalities were too competitive for that; we took turns cooking meals. Our first meeting at work was a monthly management meeting. Since he was new, we did a getting-to-know-you exercise. I had described myself as competitive, which caused him to snicker a retort, "I'm competing against you whether you know it or not." Funny and arrogant, I recalled, was my first impression of him. We had a good laugh about that months later. I thought back, trying to find a memory that would overpower the growing sadness inside me. Unfortunately, all I could remember was Bubba.

The tall, faded blue, plastic-insulated cup that had been affectionately named Bubba was the best friend who had never left his side. Unexpectedly, the day he found that cup was the day I learned he was a thief. A few years back, after dinner time, we ran to the grocery. He darted towards the paper goods, and I grabbed the juice and made my way through the checkout. He jogged up to meet me at the car, grinning. Then I saw him pull a plastic tumbler out from under his sweatshirt. He stole a stupid plastic cup with a sticker that said, Bubba.

I remembered receiving instructions on what type and how high to fill the ice, how much and what kind of vodka to add, and which juices were approved mixers. Then while visiting my parents, without warning and after three years, he suddenly switched from orange juice to cranberry juice mixers. My mother had proudly purchased the "right, no pulp brand" and, dismayed by the change, made a trip back to the grocery store just to satisfy him. It wasn't that she opted to make an additional trip; he expected her to. His entitled, slightly condescending attitude had become more noticeable to me. That should have been a red flag. His demeanor left me with a sense of dread and the urge to apologize to my mother. Instead, I thanked my mom while my gut twisted up inside me. His sudden turn of fancy was always part of his fickle nature; I had just ignored it along with the intuitive, wordless warning that was telling me something was not right. He was not the man I made him out to be in my mind.

Bubba was always lovingly hand-washed and set aside to dry. He was a star player who never sat on the bench and was in the daily starting lineup. The cup was like a sidekick on a talk show, quiet but always present. But, on the other hand, the life of the party was B. He was Mr. Five O'clock Cocktail. If it was five p.m., he had a drink in his hand. If it was Saturday and he was golfing, even at a seven a.m. start, he left with a drink in his hand and a fifth of Svedka in his golf bag. Sunday afternoon, drink in hand. Driving kids around over the shared custody weekend, drink in hand; visiting family, drink in hand. When traveling for work, his first stop was the liquor store, and yes, he took Bubba on the road. I look back and see that he so obviously had a problem.

He drank every day. I tried many times to change things, "Hey, let's take a break this week; we could go hiking, hit golf balls, or binge T.V." He'd sincerely agree and then say he forgot while cradling Bubba like a security blanket, and *I* drank with him. I always gave in and had a drink. I can justify to myself that my mixed drink was much weaker, but the truth is, I did not stand up for myself. I did not have any boundaries. "No" was not a word I could say when asked to do something, even if I didn't want to. The value I held for myself came from the reactions of others. I learned that filling the ice ⅞ of the glass, vodka to the top of the ice, and a splash of juice made him happy. I thought that made me happy.

I tried his mix on a few occasions when I felt tough or wanted to impress him, and I immediately spat it out. It was so strong that the vapors of alcohol burned my nose before I even took a drink, but once it passed my lips and made its way past the point of no return, my stomach was on fire. I coughed and choked and looked at him incredulously; he shrugged, laughing slyly, and took a long drink as he walked away and headed up to his desk, gesturing with his right hand. He waved me off and dismissed me! It was like I had lost the right to be in his presence, somehow failing his hazing. I felt compelled to try again, to pass the test, but I thought better of it. I had no idea how he finished three or more concoctions every night. If you were looking for B at 5 p.m., like clockwork, he was smoking a pack of Marlboro lights and cuddling Bubba on the patio. I followed suit. It seemed normal-ish.

● ● ●

Today was June second, my forty-fourth birthday, five weeks before the wedding, and here I sat utterly alone, abandoned, and worrying about the future. I never did well on my own; I found it unsettling. I felt guilty and selfish, but that quickly fled as the angry flames licked the thought clean from my brain. The vagueness of the future sat in front of me like a gas-filled tanker. It is about to collide and explode with the ravaging fire of my growing rage. I knew he needed help and was going to get it. I did not think he would be there for three or more months.

Searching for anything that would comfort me or take my mind off the present moment, I opened the cabinet doors one by one. I didn't just open them; I flung them open, the doors smacking the cabinet's frame. It was a satisfying sound that resonated throughout the tiny kitchen. I reached up to slap cabinet door two open, but nothing was there except the dishes. I thought of smashing them, but I just bought them and loved the deep blue and brown glazed color. Utterly dissatisfied and spoiling for a fight, I hastily moved to door three and noticed its paint-worn spot where his hands had opened it a thousand times; I was shocked.

There was Bubba.

While whipping the cabinet door open, that stupid cup seemed to wink daringly at me, and as the door whooshed passed my face to slam closed, I said, "Oh, hell no," a strong exaggeration on the "ll" sound of the word hell. I became fixated on the object as I slowly opened the door. I had spent so much time caring for Bubba: washing, drying, filling up, following ridiculous and meticulous instructions while watching him drink his life away, watching him drink our life away. I thought of how I had a few cups but never just one. Bubba was *his precious* cup. It was the closest I could get to him at this moment, and Bubba was about to meet his maker. As the explosion of rage, regret, and blame washed over and traversed through me, I threw it as hard as I could across the tiny kitchen, and after impact, I saw the impression it left in the drywall. A chunk of plaster joined the shards of plastic that exploded onto the floor. I smashed the hell out of that cup, damaged a piece of him, bits I had clung to for too long. Finally, I let go of my relationship with that cup and with liquor altogether. It felt good to be relieved of a reminder of him. Breaking that cup was a symbolic gesture that helped me claim myself back just a little. That night I moved his clothes and every piece of "him" I could find into the guest bedroom. The lingering smell of him now turned my stomach.

I was not just the girlfriend who fixed the drinks and kept him company while he got drunk or rode in the golf cart beside him while he played a round with his friends or some other role that solely bore witness. Parts that I now admitted I had accepted to feel falsely secure and loved. I had to give up trying to make him love me, to stop the chameleonic chasing of his affection. I was not responsible for his decisions either. No matter my best efforts, no amount of trying to be the perfect woman. I would never be enough for him. I could not fix the relationships he didn't have with his sons, and feeling as though I had somehow failed was now a ridiculous notion. I couldn't win; I could not control his thoughts or feelings about me. I could not stop his wandering eye; it wasn't my fault he had one. I could not make his sons forgive him for abandoning them. I had to stop trying to be what I thought he wanted; I had to be myself and if that was not enough, so be it. I needed only to be enough for myself.

In all my misplaced concerns, I had forgotten what was, in fact, mine to own. I discovered that I was the sole owner of my thoughts and feelings, and that included my reactions to the

I discovered that I was the sole owner of my thoughts and feelings, and that included my reactions to the behaviors of others.

behaviors of others. That is all I needed to be responsible for; when you think about it, that is enough for any human being to control. Damn. That realization stung like a blistering sunburn. Following the tennis ball, the notion again volleyed into my conscious brain. I could not focus on how I had gotten to this place in my life. I had gotten so dependent on other people that I didn't know what ownership of my decisions even looked like. These thoughts were too much. My subconscious mind took over, and I took a back seat. I grabbed a glass of wine, and in one gulp, it was gone, then another until the bottle was empty and my pulsating brain soothed. The score was now 30, Love, well-played subconscious. Lamenting the losing score and perplexed as to whose side my mind was on, the sounds of crunching plastic got my attention.

I snapped to the mess before me. When I thought about explaining myself or my actions to anyone who saw Bubba's remains or heard the noise, I was suddenly focused and motivated to find the dust broom. Embarrassed by my loss of self-control, I felt the shrinking and smallness returning, the sense that if he saw me this way, disappointment would emanate from his eyes. I was judging myself like I thought he would. B was a condescending man but generally of good cheer. He regarded himself as in control at all times and as the most intelligent person in any room. He would position himself as the center of attention whenever possible, masterfully manipulating his audience to fulfill his needs. No one could top his game of one-upmanship. The walls of the townhome were thin, and I realized I had let out quite a string of obscenities in the process of killing that cup. As the rage diminished, I replaced it with self-consciousness; I quickly swept up the plastic shards, threw them in the trash, and took the half-filled bag of garbage out to the curb in one smooth motion. I slipped back into the house through the side gate undetected. I heaved a sigh and realized that Bubba and B were now

MIA. It was the end of a long first day. I lumbered, rather defeatedly, up the steps to the bedroom.

● ● ●

The summers in Texas were always hot. It was the one constant that anyone in Dallas could count on, despite the ebbs and flows of traffic, soaring gas prices, or the inexplicably inconsistent availability of an avocado. If you were in Texas and it was July, it was hot as hell; the kind of heat made you tired and feel drained of all motivation. Dallas weather fluctuated between extremes. Some days the moody weather changed its mind more than a child in a candy store. Despite the triple digits for ten days straight, cooking the clay soil beyond its cries for mercy, it was day two, and I decided to take a walk.

Window shades in homes were always drawn, and people stayed inside, which made the neighborhood look deserted and the houses abandoned. If you spied a raised window shade, you couldn't help but stare and peer inside to catch the equivalent of a disappointing curiosity at a circus. The only signs of life were sprinkler systems that came on at dusk and dawn, and a few diesel-guzzling buses that labored past the townhome community entrance a block away. The neighborhood was lined with various mature trees that generously offered shade while their roots pushed relentlessly on slabs of the sidewalk, causing the concrete to crack and buckle at the edges. They seemed to get more aggressive every year. Like the world's slowest earthquake fault line, crevasses and cracks grew unevenly, and walking after dark became perilous.

In the evening, signs of life returned, and while standing on the porch, I could catch the wafting aroma of charcoal-fueled grills and sizzling beef patties. I could hear faint laughter a few doors down and screams from the children stealing the last few minutes of daylight at the playground two blocks away, and if the wind was blowing, I could smell an intoxicating sweet Olive tree. This tree was half a block over, and its fragrance would tickle and delight my nose. I waited until most dog walkers and joggers finished their routes to venture out.

I loved walking past that yard at dusk, it smelled so intoxicatingly good, and the setting sun threw off brilliant shades of red, purple, and faded orange. I would linger there, breathing in a few deep whiffs, straining to get closer to the blooms without looking conspicuous, and trying to soak in the colors of the sky was a great use of time as B was on the road traveling for work several days every week. Then, I realized I probably looked weird sniffing a tree in a stranger's yard. Still, one last deep breath of sweet floral magic while simultaneously checking for anyone who might be looking out their window was worth it. Reluctantly, I moved on before I got caught and questioned. I headed for the sanctuary of home.

● ● ●

As the rays of intense summer sun rose to meet and surpass the uncovered half-circle window, my swollen and sore eyes felt assaulted. It was day three. I reached for my phone, rubbed out the sleep, and saw there was a voicemail from him. The Arizona area code got my attention. I had missed his call, and as I replayed the message, a fresh flood of anxiety overwhelmed me. He said he had arrived in southern Arizona, and as the cab left him at the facility, he thought of making a run for it. His voice sounded weak, frail, and shaky. Fear was a state I had never seen him in. Finally, he confessed that the last day he went without a drink was nearly a decade ago. Some quick math revealed the startling statistic that he drank for over three thousand five hundred consecutive days.

There had been something vast bubbling under the surface for decades, long before we met, and for a moment, I was ashamed of my reaction to the first time he said the words "re" and "hab" in the same sentence. He used to joke that rehab is for quitters. The slow suicide of his best friend had shaken him to the core. Since childhood, he had known a man who had been like a brother and drank himself to death. Secretly rejecting a liver transplant sealed his fate, and he was found dead of liver failure eight weeks before he was part of the wedding party. B was an attention-seeking man who was replaced with a sorrowful shell of himself, worrying about his future and the damage he had done to his liver. At the time, he announced his intentions to get help. I was proud of his decision. Sarcastically, I said under my breath, "it's about time," and then, more faintly, a despairing little voice in my mind said, "weddings off." My thoughts would drift to the uncertain future, and I did anything, and everything I could think of to stay distracted until the reassuring call I was hoping for would come. With every passing minute, that call slipped farther away.

As day three progressed, I was surprised to get a phone call from my mom. Right off the bat, I knew something was up. Her tone was unsteady and confused. I could tell she was uncomfortable, and as she inquired about the owner of an email address, the hairs on my neck stood up. Why was his sister sending my parents an email? This had never happened before. Waves of panic started to build; whatever this message was, it could not be good. I told her to send it to me, and I would open it as they didn't have the right software to open the attachment. Once it hit my inbox, I feverishly opened it and dropped right to the sofa after the first sentence. I realized he broke up with me via a letter to my mom and dad. His "always remember us this way" message now made more sense. The feelings of rage, sadness, and betrayal were flooding the inbox of my mind and heart, followed quickly by fear.

His lengthy letter urged my father to "save his little girl." He was convinced his leaving would cause me to commit suicide. According to B, ending the relationship, forcing me to leave my home, and canceling the wedding five weeks away would be too much for me to survive. My demise would only be prevented by my parents rescuing me immediately. Instead, he wove a tapestry of excuses and deflected all responsibility. My mind was spinning. Was that his goodbye to me? Seven and a half years, and I got a post-it note, a movie quote, and a re-used framed picture. In my mind, I called him every name in the book.

In the letter, he shared my skeletons. These secrets had transformed themselves into knives. They were shiny and sharp little daggers; each remark a betrayal. He lodged all of them firmly in my back. I was given four weeks to find a new place to live, instructed to move out, told to cancel every aspect of the wedding, close every account, ordered to break the lease, and prepare his possessions for relocation, which were to be picked up by his mother. After I retrieved my jaw off the floor, I nearly threw up as the wave of panic rushed through me, like a drop from the world's tallest roller coaster, flipping my guts up into my throat and the sheer terror at the thought of my father and mother reading this letter was too much. I grabbed my phone and dialed the house. My mother answered, and my first words were, "Whatever you do, don't open it. Please, delete the letter." She hadn't heard me clearly because she excitedly stated, "Your father is reading it now; we got it open."

"Fuuuuuuuuhhhhhhck. Me." I hung up. I screamed in rage until blood vessels in my face burst. For the first time, I did not care what the neighbors would think, I did not care if anyone heard, and I did not care that the tears caused my make-up to run. I simply could not reconcile what was happening; I was short-circuiting. Then, when I didn't think it could get worse, that he could not find another way to hurt me or humiliate me, he did. I saw the date on the letter, topping off this all-you-can-eat buffet of B's bullshit. I tried to focus my eyes to see if I was mistaken; I looked at my phone, confirming the last insult to injury. It was dated the day before he left for rehab. *He knew all along*, and *this was* **his plan**. He had lied about everything. He never intended to get married or even stay together. Like superheated mercury, my anger burst the thermometer of my body. I grabbed the nearest object and launched it without considering its trajectory or target. "Son of a bitch!" I yelled. Glass shattered and rained down onto the wooden floor, again and again; I destroyed whatever was within reach. No matter what I broke, it did not change a damn thing.

As I fumbled around for something to blow my nose with, I suddenly laughed out loud, watery snot dripping from my nostrils. This was a laugh of mania—a high-pitched cackling. So there I stood, crying, laughing, nose dripping, no tissue, make-up smeared, and unable to look at myself.

"Holy shit Miller, get it together," I shouted unsteadily. I couldn't stop going from one extreme response to the next; this must be a nervous breakdown. What did I do to deserve this? I felt a deep sense of guilt and shame, and fear. I thought, "How could he throw me away? Am I just a piece of garbage... I am just a piece of garbage." I spoke it out loud, and the image of a speck of lint being flicked off hit me like a punch in the gut. I imagined a bottle cap with a miniature portrait of my smiling face printed on it aggressively flicked aside. I felt like garbage. Left alone and exposed like a beetle on its back, I admitted I picked the wrong man... again. Damn you, B, and damn me.

When I saw myself as nothing but garbage, I hit bottom. I knew this pit well; I have lived in it. I tried clinging to some shred of hope he would be back and want me. But, I was telling myself a lie. I had to change my thinking.

I will be ok because I am enough and worthy of Love. Those words felt better, somehow more authentic but foreign. They seemed like a dream I was trying to recall. I repeated them over and over. I took that afternoon minute by minute. I was deflated but not defeated. I knew the feeling of barely holding.

In my teenage years, I resorted to self-harm, cutting to be precise, to exert control. I felt a strong urge to do it now, but I could not take steps backward. The past was dead. I needed to leave that behavior buried. Glad to be alone in the dark. I prayed quietly, like a sincere child. Instead of begging God for something, I began to think of what was good in my life. It took a while to flip the script. I found a few things, then a few more. Finally, surprised, I felt a little better.

●　●　●

At 22, I married D. The relationship became verbally, emotionally, and physically abusive. My confidence and self-esteem have been issues, and those weaknesses were used against me. I allowed myself to fall prey to the addiction of being needed. I traded my desires, likes, and hobbies for a false sense of security. The fifteen years I stayed in the marriage were fourteen and three quarters too long. I was determined to heal him and fix the relationship; after all, I was no quitter. Focusing on my well-being and self-care had not yet occurred to me. What I needed to do was know myself and reprogram the way I felt about myself. I couldn't comprehend that fear and weak-mindedness were what kept me from seeing the obvious. He became a cruel man who used isolation and religion to break me down until there was nothing of me left. I gave away all I was, desperately trying to be what he wanted. He was prone to fits of rage, violence, interrogation, and abuse. Not many even consider being raped by your spouse a crime, so I never said anything or reported it. That was his gift for my twenty-eighth birthday.

Through repeated abuse, he planted a clone-like seed of himself inside my mind so that when he wasn't there, his voice was. He would hold his hands on my wrists like a human lie detector. His accusatory and hurtful words made a home in my head. His hatred was now there, and it was insidiously disguised as self-loathing. I hated myself. No wonder there was a rebirth necessary to survive it. How else could I start again? I had to become someone new. After two years of therapy, I finally rid myself of that deeply rooted evil seed. Ripping it out, root and stem, and casting it away saved my soul. I did not know what I wanted; I just did not want to be treated that way anymore. I have never been short on two things, talent or insecurity.

Had I stayed any longer, D would have killed me. He hated me with a deep-seated intensity that could only be repackaged and sold to the unwilling-to-see woman I was, as Love. Capital "L" love. I Loved with all the energy and might that I had until there was nothing left. Ironically, one of the last things he ever said to me was, "You are such a stuck-up mid-western bitch, you only care about yourself... the gun's on the nightstand." I will never forget the longest eight steps I took to clear the bathroom and bedroom. He stood with his arms on both sides of the bathroom doorway. I ducked under his arm and saw the pistol. It was lying there, black, shiny, and winking at me. The clip full of 9MM hollow point ammunition was locked securely in the pistol grip, and as I exited the room, I saw the safety was off. I thought, "I've got a fifty-

fifty chance he's gonna shoot me in the back." But, I *had* to go; as I left for work four hours early, eager to get to a safe place, I prayed again. I gathered all my strength, breathed deeply, and took those steps.

At that point, I did not care. I accepted the odds and walked purposefully yet, a little meekly, the remaining twenty-three steps it took to get from the bedroom doorway to the front door, through the carport, and in one smooth motion, on my twenty-third step, I slipped into the driver's seat of my car. I noticed I was violently shaking when I locked the doors. Looking up to the front porch for D, I saw the sad and hurt look in my dog's eyes instead as I struggled to get the key in the ignition. My heart broke. Then the memory of being picked up by my neck lifted off the ground, and thrown across the room by D rushed over me, and I mouthed the words I'm sorry to my now abandoned pets. D was not a big guy. What gave him strength was wrath. Bitter disdain at everything and everyone, especially his mother, for being born. The hole in him was so big that all the love in the world would not be enough to fill it. What he hungered for was worship and codependency. No human being could satisfy that desperate appetite.

I had traded everything I owned, every bit of freedom, self-worth, sanity, safety, and nearly my life for what I thought was love. He could not fix me either. It wasn't Love; it was manipulation, emotional, physical, and sexual abuse fueled by rage, ignorance, poverty, fear, insecurity, jealousy, and a massive dash of shame and embarrassment. That was the nightmare we called marriage.

> I had traded everything I owned, every bit of freedom, self-worth, sanity, safety, and nearly my life for what I thought was love.

I was starting to take ownership of my thoughts and emotions. When I thought about the strength it took to leave D after fifteen years, to take twenty-three steps with a loaded pistol at your back and never to look back, to leave with nothing but the clothes on your back, I was proud of that woman. I tried to channel that strength all these years later and found it was disappointingly out of reach. Because it seemed in my mind to have happened to another young woman, a technique I think I employed as a coping mechanism, I could not draw upon it. I could not claim the strength without feeling the pain; that is the price I am paying for putting her on the shelf of life experiences. She was now a stranger to me, and she, too, was alone. Could we become acquainted again, should we?

●　●　●

I had somehow managed the medicated, deliberate, and delicate balance of emotional and spiritual sleepwalking through my life while; simultaneously experiencing the hurt, fear, sorrow, shame, and guilt of the people in my surroundings. The puzzling polarity was not lost on my intellect. If I heard someone make that claim, I wouldn't believe it. How was that duality even possible? But, taking my attention to my heart, I could hardly hear or feel it beating. The walls around my feelings were so dense with scar tissue that only the most significant highs and lows could pass. My Gemini, air-cooled supercomputer of a mind, set free thoughts that moved at the speed of light. My body, no matter how once athletic, lagged pitifully behind the rate of my mind. Somehow, I was ripping that scar tissue out. This letter, this moment in time, humiliating betrayal, the sheer loss of everything I knew tore down the fortress. Just like the seed had been torn out, so followed the collapse of the wall around my heart.

In the past, I would walk or run right off the cliff of reason and get lost in depression, negative thoughts, self-loathing, and taking responsibility for those around me. I played the martyr well. I have always truly cared about people and would help anyone in any way I could, but this was different. This behavior was making me a martyr in my mind, not for the benefit of being seen by others. I had no idea how to block the strong feelings I felt from those around me and still feel my own. I had to figure out how to take on only the emotions that belonged to me.

This time I was pushed off the cliff, and I didn't know how to get back. That breeze I felt was me falling from what little grace I had. And again exhausted, utterly spent, I fell into a fitful and dark, dream-filled slumber. Even in sleep, I knew no comfort at this time. I awoke enough to see it was still dark, drenched in sweat. I peeled off the pajamas I had put on a few hours ago. I tested my theory that this was all a dream; checking my phone, I saw it staring at me. From the inbox with its judging glow, that letter happened. Everything had gone to shit. I put the phone down without opening it. The words were not going to change. Leaving the soggy clothes on the floor, I crawled to the dry side of the bed and slept.

I was unaware that what woke me up were several missed calls from my mom and dad. I gathered myself up, went downstairs, grabbed a Coke, and dialed the house. With what little courage I could muster, I said, "Hi, Dad, I'm so sorry about all this." My hands and voice were shaky. He responded as I should have known he would, with loving-kindness and just the right amount of "F- that guy. Peanut, I know who you are." It was the first sliver of something good. A serving of Love, of being known and accepted, of credit given for work done and was received by a deeper part of myself. It was a tiny spark of light in a very dark place. Talking to my father, I felt better; he clarified his reaction, thoughts, and feelings, which were consoling to me. His life experience gave him a window into the kind of disappointment and pain I felt.

He reassured me that, after all we had been through as a family, he saw right through that letter and was relieved that I was free of someone who would not be a good partner.

Through my mother's tears shed for the hurt I was feeling, I knew that she would want nothing more than to hug me. She, too, understood betrayal, tough decisions, and taking ownership of one's actions. Her strength and fierce loyalty would become a source of inspiration for me. I didn't know it then, but my family would evolve into the rock I would lean on repeatedly over the next several months and years. I got to know each family member more personally, not just by their role. Either my soul made a good choice, or I was fortunate because my entire family was an incredible blessing. The Love I received lives on. To know me and be accepted as me, even just a little, felt terrific.

The fear of judgment subsided slightly, and I began to plot just what I wanted to say to B on the inevitable call. I had to get a chance to say something. I could not have meant so little that I didn't even get one phone call. He had planned his exit perfectly, a Houdini-style-let-everyone-else-clean-up-my-mess exit. Well played, B. But there were two boys, his sons from previous relationships, that were now off-limits; I was sure he hadn't thought of that even once. I would never see them graduate school, go to college, or grow into men and get married. No goodbye to the little boy I had known since he was two and a half.. What about the older boy, so sensitive? Would they miss me at all? Would their memories of me be kind? Would they remember the Love I have for them? I was going to miss those boys. I bet he never even thought about how *they* would feel. Another wave of anger welled up, but I was too tired to do anything with it. I curled up on the couch with the tv on, not wanting to sleep in the room that still was full of his smell.

* * *

Day five, still nothing from him. I felt everything slipping away. I had nothing to move towards, just standing on a shoreline alone, watching the imaginary raft that held me and everything I knew drifting aimlessly away. I thought of setting it all ablaze like a Viking funeral. Off to Valhalla with you!

My brother, five years my senior, was kind enough to come down and stay for a few days. Poor guy, I could barely get a few words out without tears. He was not the most comfortable with his little sister's girly tears, but he said, "How much money do you have saved?" It was then that our conversation led to the notion of home ownership. He said with a smile, "Let's make a plan."

As a realtor, he knew the process, and surprisingly, I might be able to buy something. Me, a homeowner? The thought danced in my mind, a sugar plum fairy of a notion, a long-held desire, a dream. Could this one come true? My brother and I formulated a lengthy checklist of things to do. Working steadily down the list, I felt less overwhelmed and genuinely grateful. Our age difference meant he was in high school and heading for college by the time I passed the annoying little sister stage. When he graduated, I had already moved out of state. We were always missing each other, and while we weren't strangers, we weren't as close as I would have liked. I couldn't put my finger on why, but having him there brought us together in a way that permanently cemented my big brother as my friend and someone I admire and respect. His cheerful demeanor helped me get through the days, one at a time. We spent Day six focused on homeownership.

Day seven, and my brother's skills were in full force. He interviewed a local realtor, had a list of documents and questions for me, and had already made an appointment. It was impressive, so no shock when he headed to bed early. Then my phone rang from a number with an Arizona area code. This was it, the call I had been anticipating. My heart was pounding in my chest; I felt flush and anxious. I felt like pacing, but instead, I took the phone outside with me to the patio, took a deep breath, then another, and answered nonchalantly.

"Hello?" I said.

"Hey, how's it going?" he said with nervous confidence. I could tell he had prepared for this phone call giving him the upper hand, the high ground.

"Fine," I said, "Got your letter, or rather my mom and dad did. Hey, Thanks for that."

I couldn't help the sarcasm and disdain. B knew I would not appreciate the letter sent to my parents, but he felt sure I would have a breakdown and claimed to have done it out of concern. My mind immediately called bullshit on that, and I felt the heat of anger swelling. When had he done anything for anyone other than for himself?

He didn't know that when I read the letter, I steeled myself to keep it together to spite him and prove to everyone I knew I could hold it together. I would not melt down. I would not break, not in any way that he would see. I also had an ace up my sleeve, one I could throw in his face. I wanted him to hurt, to know I was not a doormat. I mattered. He tried to keep the conversation banal, going over the practical checklist of what fell under my purview.

He expected me to sever ties and clean up the mess he left behind. He expected me to take care of every detail to make it easy for him.

"No," I mouthed the word as he kept talking. "No," I said loud enough for him to hear. He was confused, "No, what?" he said.

"No, is a perfectly acceptable answer; I am not doing all that; it's not my job. I don't care what happens. You have thrown me out of an airplane at fifty-thousand feet without a parachute," I said, my voice rising in pitch and intensity.

He warned me that he would hang up unless I could be calm. But, unfortunately, that warning made it worse; my face flushed red with a sorrow-filled rage causing my heart to pound, shoulders to tense, and fists to clench. The desire to vengefully hurt him, to be consoled, and to hear him admit why he threw me away fought like wild cats shaken in a suitcase.

"Did you *ever* love me?" I said, the question hanging in the air.

"Yes, I did, I still do, I was killing myself, and I had to change. And, I don't know who I will be or how long this will take, and I cannot save myself *and you.*"

I heard his words, but the "save me" part shut down my rational mind, the vengeful fighter claiming victory. "I never asked you to or **needed you** to save me! I am not the one that drank for four thousand consecutive days," I replied defiantly.

I went further, thinking this was an excellent time to play my ace. "If you were so in love with me and wanting to saaave me," I exaggerated the words, "why were you sleeping with some woman in California at your friend's wake!" Then, finally, I spat the last few words out.

"That is NOT love," I spat out. Game, set, match, I thought.

His stepmother spilled the beans about his infidelity, hoping to console me. I was anything but. Instead, it was a humiliating realization that I had been asleep at the wheel of my life.

His retort was short, "How'd you find out? It doesn't matter, I did; I am sorry you heard about that. I am being treated for sex addiction too," his voice lowered, whispering the last words. I was sure he could hear my eye roll.

"You are just too **good** for me; you are the best person I know," were his last words. I lost it; tears and every emotion came pouring out, and at that moment, he hung up and was out of my life forever.

Was that closure? Was that the end? After a few minutes, I wiped my face off on my shirt and left the back porch; I walked to the bathroom. I was glad that was over; I never have to see him again, I was relieved.

Flipping on the light, I surveyed my face, nose, ears, curly hair, skin, and mouth and gazed deeply into my eyes. Looking past the flecks of green, blue, and gold. I felt a stirring inside. I could only imagine it was my soul looking at me, observing without judgment. It was like she was waiting for me to see her and smiled at me when I did. I told her; I am sorry I had put us through this again. I am sorry I keep looking to others for my sense of self-worth. I am sorry that I am always sorry. I am empty, and I don't want to be.

I wanted to feel fulfilled. I wanted to love myself. It was the first time in a long time that I thought about how I felt about myself. "Jen, I love you," I whispered the words; it sounded fake and silly. So, I repeated it. I kept declaring it for years until it stuck, even a little.

What do I do now, and how do I go on? What do I want? The questions came rapidly, without answers, but there was no desire to push them away, which was very different. It was the first time in a long time that I saw myself not in comparison to others, not in competition with the world, not desperate to please everyone, not giving all of myself away. Instead, my soul offered what remained of me a tiny bit of tenderness. The little girl so eager to please, singing silly songs and fearlessly flipping and tumbling, was long gone. The young woman who unwittingly trapped herself in a cycle of unhealthy relationships in which she kept no boundaries and lost herself was finally waving goodbye.

It would be a long road, in fact, a never-ending journey, but seeing me at that moment started a chain reaction of profound transformation. It was like splitting the atom; unlimited energy was released, and Powerful reserves of Love, creativity, passion for life, and gratitude for everything I had experienced and learned became the thoughts and feelings that replaced doubt and fear. I saw that the path to my happiness lay within me, not out in the world, nor was it the responsibility of the person I was with to make me whole. I could not shake the feeling; it was so different than anything I had felt before. I tried to paint and draw how I felt and the image of a Phoenix bird rising emerged. That symbol captured my life's eternal journey and the neverending path to know myself. Life became an adventure again. That night I felt a subtle sense of peace lying in bed. I took a deep breath, another, and a third…as I exhaled and closed my eyes, I knew I would get rest, even if just a little, because now, I had a sliver of hope.

As the days and weeks progressed, the date of the now-canceled wedding was upon me. I was going to take the trip to meet my family at the location. My aunt and uncle, several years back, had purchased a bed and breakfast that they kept for family, religious retreats, and guests. It is a beautiful place with a heated pool, tennis court, hot tub, and access to a sandy beach, home to a lighthouse and a mere fifty feet from the shores of a bay off Lake Michigan. It's my favorite place to go. The glass A-frame was spacious with three bedrooms, three and a half baths, and a wrap-around porch surrounded by pine trees. My family filled up every room. As the caravan of cars arrived, I felt a little like an insect under a microscope, but I knew that if there was anywhere, I could relax, it was here. I got oodles of hugs, and there was much bustling and shuffling about, claiming rooms, unpacking, and organizing before a late dinner. I had so many eyes on me that I needed a moment to myself. I walked to the garage just a few feet away; hopping on the leather seat, I took the golf cart out. As I backed out, the cart beeping angrily, I yelled to my dad, "I'm going to the lighthouse; I'll be back in a bit." I put it in drive, stomped on the gas, and pulled away.

The cool air felt good on my face, and despite the occasional bug hitting my skin, I kept up the quick speed. It was nearly dark, so I hit the light on the cart and kept going until I reached the beach. Turning off the golf cart and leaving the key, I headed to the beach path. The sand swallowed my sneaker-covered feet, and I could feel the grains filling up my shoes. One hundred yards further to go, and there it was, a beautiful, old, bright-red lighthouse and coast guard station. The giant bulb atop the tower circled dutifully. I remembered the many times I had been here before. Today felt different.

Finally, I reached the concrete inlet and climbed on. The breaker stretched out a good one hundred feet. The last shred of the sun was just slipping below the horizon and the moon was rising. I was amazed at the number of stars I could see from here. Besides a few lights on the beach and the lighthouse beacon, it was dark. The mosquitoes were finding me now as the wind had died down, and I lingered there just a moment more. The waves lapped upon the breakers and the shore. I could smell the water, feel its flow and rhythm, and as my thoughts floated by, I got a sense of stillness. I realized it was coming from inside of me. For once, my mind, so prone to racing, was still, my body at rest and not twitching with unused energy. I felt at peace more than just the kind you get when you plop into a chair and sigh in relief. A real profound connection formed between my conscious mind and my inner being. It felt good being with my family. Coming home to myself felt safe and long overdue.

I didn't realize at the time that the stillness I experienced was actually meditating. Whenever I had tried to in the past, my body fidgeted and my mind fought me. I was convinced I was doing it wrong. This was different; I was letting go. I gave up trying to control everything. Stopping my thoughts was impossible; I just had to breathe and watch them flow by, not engaging my inner dialogue. "Just keep breathing," I told myself. I knew for the first time that letting go of the past hurts and mistakes was the way to get through the darkness, grow, and find the light within. I was connecting to something profound, beautiful, and universal. The world's collective consciousness was immense; my voice was part of it and growing louder. This stillness was found in the now, the present moment. The past is only to be learned from, I thought. I have to let it go, I cannot change it. I found peace with where and who I was, and ignited my curiosity about the world around me. Turning my energy and attention to this transformation and sharing my story was how I would heal.

My consciousness was waking up now. When I opened my eyes to be in the moment and not trapped in a loop of negative thoughts, the stars were brighter, and the air was sweeter. "This is my place," I told myself. "I claim it for my own, and I humbly thank the powers above for this gift. I love it here," I spoke out loud, clearly, and authentically. "Thank you for seeing me, for this life, and please continue to know me and guide me on my path," and a smile crossed my face. I did not know where the words came from, but they felt right. My heart felt bright, my eyes clear, and all my senses acutely aware it was about to rain. I ran back to the golf cart, hit the gas, and sped back. I was dumping the sand out of my shoes just as the sky opened up, and it poured a soothing and purifying rain. Heavy drops pelted my exposed skin. It was quenching the angry flames that had uncontrollably burnt my heart. Grabbing my shoes, I ran towards the sliding doors. Before ducking inside, I glanced to my left to see the tall pine and maple trees swaying in the wind. It seemed as though they were waving to me, celebrating this newfound wisdom. I was relieved, re-energized, and felt like I was standing on solid ground, ready for the next leg of life's journey.

I rushed to hug my parents, and I felt Joy. I remembered how much I Loved that feeling. This place felt holy and time with my family was a gift. Then, Love began to emanate from inside, and that was different. Hope and Joy seemed to flow from a light-filled well in my chest.

"I am enough," I cried out. These were three words I had not previously spoken or felt, but they would become a mantra that resonated profoundly, and would help heal me. I had never realized that the limit to how sincerely we can Love another is in direct relationship and proportion to how thoroughly and absolutely we forgive ourselves. Healing could only be superficial until I could face my mistakes head-on without excuses and take ownership of my thoughts and emotions. Remembering all the faces that have shared even a single step on their path with me, I can report there is no shortcut or circumventing of forgiving and loving yourself. Your love for someone else cannot replace our relationship with ourselves, no matter how hard we try.

● ● ●

After months of telling myself that "I love you, I am enough, I am proud of you," as I looked at myself in the mirror, I would come to feel it. I let go of what no longer served me. When I got to the point of believing, I started to expect. I expected good things to happen, for what I thought about and put my energy behind could become my reality. I pushed away negative thoughts; negative people no longer ate up my time. I said "no," when appropriate, creating boundaries. I put myself first. Before anyone or anything else, the time I needed was my priority. Although I felt selfish at first, it soon felt natural. I had more energy, clarity, and time to give.

Then I made a list of goals and adopted a quote about success that resonated with me deeply. I kept thinking about what the world considered a successful person, and while money means freedom, it does not guarantee fulfillment.

"Success is the progressive realization of a worthy ideal."

What were my values, and what did I stand for? I had to know myself better to discover my purpose. So I invested in tools to dig deeper, to understand my personality, strengths, weaknesses, tendencies, patterns of behavior, and skills. When I understood who I was and what my gifts were and accepted that I was not made broken. I was divinely created and I began living by faith. It was then that real miracles began to happen and still happen every day.

I'm as unique as you, no more, no less. Yet, we are the same. I am you; you are me. I embrace all of me and, therefore, all of you without judgment, and I offer the gift of listening and knowing you for all you are. That is how we Love and heal. We are one; our free will separates us, but our souls are intertwined. Sharing this story and this simple and profound lesson that has saved my soul has delivered me to my life's purpose.

Look inward for your Love, value, and identity. Look inward to know yourself and Love all you see with all your might. Every human being has the possibility of experiencing Joy and Love. The journey starts with being still, knowing yourself, and being grateful for who and where you are. Cultivate sincere gratitude for the lessons you have learned no matter how painful, and I promise that as the sun rises, the rain will come, the stars twinkle, and you will find your path and live with Love for yourself and others, and you'll experience your Joy. I never thought I could, but as I prepare for my upcoming wedding to the man of my dreams, who exhibits all the qualities I wrote on my list of goals for my perfect partner, I say resoundingly, "Yes! Yes, you can!"

Your scars and suffering serve as no credentials here,

Save your worldly repartee; forbidden is all false cheer.

Make no home in your body, mind, or soul for pain, hurt or hate.

Know thyself as divine, make the body a temple, your mind a gate.
Walk with me, fly beside me, conquer the nagging flames of
doubt and dread.

Open your eye, follow my light, show me your scars, cast off all that's dead.

Proclaim with fervor and deep gratitude, for you, shining soul,
have more than survived.

Go now! Claim your life! Joy and Love are laid bare;
truth and purpose are for you to find.

Jen Miller

Jen Miller is a successful entrepreneur, published author, professional astrologer, retired gymnastics champion, and game night enthusiast. She has dedicated her life to learning, self improvement, the mystic arts, expressions of creativity, and the pursuit of purpose so that she may be of service to others in each personal and professional interaction and project.

Jen brings a lifetime of honing her communication skills, active listening, and studying the human condition along with over twenty years of retail where she worked for some of the worlds most beloved brands, had a front row seat to every type of human interaction, studied relationship, conflict resolution, leadership and earned a Bachelor's degree in Business Leadership.

Her colorful art, published works, and speeches will leave you feeling full of love, joy and gratitude in only the way she can. As a soul born with Venus out of bounds, she has enough love to share with the entire world and the drive, desire and fortitude to walk her path and accompany you on your journey inward.

CONNECT WITH JEN

 @generalmilz    phoenix-workforce.com

CHAPTER 11

Fluffy Flakes

By Joy Danner Lehman

Fluffy flakes of snow had started falling from the sky earlier the night before. They kept coming so beautifully and gently, as though a backdrop of peaceful beauty floating down from heaven to calm and comfort us as we readied for this transition from life on earth to life with Christ, the angels, and his ancestors. Frozen particles of holy water dropped from the clouds onto the house and yard around us. The quiet created what felt like a blanket of peace and love. Possibly a dusting of welcome from heaven. My dad had prepared to die as he had lived. Love, dignity, resilience, and resolve had led and sustained him through unexpected and terminal illness towards his pending death from Esophageal Cancer. Just months before, he had joked with me on what would be his last birthday. "Sixty-seven and closer to heaven." He had been right about the fact that most wouldn't think his line was funny. We had laughed it off together, finding the mind saving humor in the irrational.

It was part of his story unfolding as he had imagined while reading the Book of Revelations, talking to his closest friends and family, and considering if unicorns were real. He wondered whether he would meet

Moses, Elijah or Abraham Lincoln, and if he did, would Elijah's hair be white and would Abe be wearing his hat. He contemplated and shared his ideas of his heavenly future during our sacred conversations. I was grateful to be a part of those ponderings.

Like a pregnancy with a due date, yet a story still untold, there we were and life as we knew it, was coming to an end. There were no words.

It seemed like a normal weekday, laying in bed with everyone still safe and cozy sleeping. Alarms were set, and the fluffy snow came down on that late November morning dark and early before dawn. I had made it through another night of restless sleep, with the weight of the world on my shoulders and the irritation and volume of a small mouse trapped and flipping around in the low ceiling attic space next to my room playing in my head. The phone rang and it startled me. My mom was on the line. "You better come now. I gave him morphine at midnight and it won't be long now," she said. I groggily hung up and woke my husband. We were quick to get out of bed in response. We got dressed without much talk or anything but robotic motions that would get us out the door so that we could be there for his departure. The impending loss was palatable. So many thoughts of logistics ran through my mind as I readied. Who would be the parent while we were the children? I'd be away from my students and the structure of a regular work day. I called in my absence and wondered when I'd return to the kids and coworkers that had kept me going with routine and daily humor for this part of the journey.

My dad's beautiful granddaughters slept peacefully in their beds. It felt reassuring to know that they would be cozy and safe while their dad and I would be at his bedside around the corner just up the street. The familiar two blocks to my childhood home.

We made the tough decision and left the girls to sleep until their alarms would go off. As a first and a fifth grader, it felt strange, but they would be ok as we locked them securely in the house with trusted neighbors close by. It would be a few hours until they would need to be ready to catch the school bus. The more rest they could get, the better it would be for them. Knowing that the kids were safe and in their own routines would reassure them and us. I had so many things on my mind as I sandwiched between the young living and the sick dying.

It seemed silly to drive the two blocks to my parent's home, yet that's exactly what we did on this early morning before daylight and through the snow. As we pulled into the driveway the snow continued. The house looked sad. This would be no ordinary stop by visit.

So many memories ran through my head. Thirty seven years prior, my dad's own dad, my grandpa, had passed away at age fifty-seven from an aggressive cancer, three and a half years after diagnosis. Another family man went too young. I had never forgotten the look of sorrow through tears on my dad's face as he left his parent's home that traumatic day. I was a little girl of only six and he was a young thirty-year-old, anticipating his third child with my newly pregnant mom still in her twenties. I had sat impatiently in the back seat of my parent's Chevy Impala in my grandparent's driveway under the crab apple tree. My three-year-old sister didn't understand as she jumped up and down waiting to find out why we had to sit in the car while our parents went inside. My dad had been paged while at the local shopping mall. My grandpa had died, and my dad and my grandma and his loyal dog Rex were so sad. I missed the funeral and remembered being left home with the neighbor lady, sick in bed, vomiting, and not realizing at the time that I was physically purging the emotional grief I had been holding in my sweet little stomach.

My grandpa's buddy had told me the church was full. Another man, who I didn't know, had told me that my grandpa was a good man. I would come to understand that comment much later after wondering what he meant. My grandpa was my God Father, so I knew that we had a special connection through God and that I would miss my time with him. From that point on, my grandma lived as a widow without her husband in their home. The special bond between her and me continued to blossom with overnights, her pets, late night tv, pro bowling, bird watching, red licorice, and her cigarettes.

Fast-forward twenty-seven years after my grandpa's death and shortly after my grandma's stroke, that same home had eventually become our little family's home after my grandma's passing and shortly after my husband and I were married. We had added our own beloved dog, Bess, and our babies. So many angels, and good spirits with layers of protection and love from the past generations in our home. That trekked path between those two places had been well worn with the family ties of love by walks and bike rides.

Little did I know who I would become or how I would grow as I walked into the room together with my mom, my siblings, and my dad's dear friend. I knew it would be the last time we would see my dad alive. The room where we would all say our final goodbyes. There was no coffee that morning. No warm welcome. No words remembered. Maybe a feeling of stunned, quiet shock or resolve. The day that I would transition from a loyal daughter and friend, mother of his granddaughters, and his coworker, to a member of the unwanted fraternal order of The Dead Dad's Club, had not crossed my mind. I would survive the day, while he would not. Life as we knew it would never be the same.

Cancer had ravaged his body and transformed him from a lifelong athlete and fit man to a small vision of his former

I would survive the day, while he would not. Life as we knew it would never be the same.

self. Questions of the future bounced in my head as I contemplated what our connection would be. *Would I feel his spiritual presence in the many places we had shared? In the wind, in the church through the communion where we connected heaven and earth through the sacrament and gifts? Up north at the lake in the woods? Was the spirit of my dog who had crossed the rainbow bridge to be found where my dad was going and if so would she have on her collar?*

As I walked into my parent's bedroom, I knew everything was about to change. I had said goodbye to friends and grandparents, as I had arrived after their passing, but I had not been part of the "surrounded by their loving family" as stated in so many obituaries. Over the years I had served on the altar at church as an acolyte and a torchbearer, sung and served as a deaconess at funerals and in the choir, and I had honored the dead on All Saint's Day. I had looked into the faces of grieving families. I had felt the mystery of it all in the communion with those saints but I hadn't watched someone take their last breath. I hadn't watched someone die.

I hadn't been there to say those last important things. Until this day of intense quiet and looming loss. I would evolve from the teacher, the supervisor, the coach's daughter, to the eldest ancestor. Being one of three and the oldest, I would be the eldest of my dad's family legacy at age forty-three. Strange. I would remember special memories with my dad, his parents, his grandma and her sisters, his aunt and uncle, his great aunt and uncle, all who had passed so long ago and before others were able to have the same memories. My dad had no siblings and I had no cousins. It was one of his life's regrets. Today, he would not be alone and neither would I. We were all with him and God was in the room. The spirit was almost visible. I could feel it in my bones and in my awkward, limited ability to express anything at all.

I would try to do the right thing without a recipe or any experience for the right way to do things. I wondered how this would go. My role was yet unknown.

We had reached the lowest point after eighteen months and weeks of the descending rollercoaster ride, seatbelts on, and this day, the lowering ups and downs would come to a complete stop. A year and a half. Well past the original twelve months or so prognosis of this life upsetting, inevitable ride through un-survivable cancer. I had never been on such a short long ride. While many others were living strong through it at the time, that was not to be his destiny. His body had wasted away and the grieving had continued from the beginning of so many phases through this disease and all of the ripples. His overall excellent health seemed to extend his days through the challenge. I had always heard him say, "When the going gets tough, the tough get going."

That said, he resembled a person twice his age and was unrecognizable to some. He had fought the hard fight, like the Battle of The Bulge as he had discussed with his oncologist. His young heart and soul were disguised by his wasting body. They were still huge and loving, though not visible and were still felt in the presence of his spirit by those who already missed his physical strength.

Eighteen months filled with choosing doctors, getting to know nurses, scheduling as well as treatment plans of radiation rounds, chemotherapy mixtures, metastasized spreading, broken bones, psychological adjustment, follow-up appointments, update reports, new prescriptions and meds, transfusions, falls, bruises, hospitalizations, and more Dr's appointments, transportation, and insurance issues. Our family and his friends had rallied around him with support. I had kept my conversations with him as separate from the health updates as possible. I didn't need to hear every medical update. He didn't need to share one more repeated report. It was so wearing.

Our talks were focused on better things. The day's events, my kids, education topics, given our shared time in the schools, and skiing and our ski friends and coworkers. He was the one that had always helped me make sense as I contemplated life's dynamics. He was the one that had apologized for his overly aggressive discipline in my early years and I had forgiven him. His situation had brought out the tender side of my compassion. Now there wasn't enough time to anticipate life without him as our rock, our family leader, our dad, our friend. Not enough time to talk about everything, to adjust, to say goodbye.

Thank goodness there would be no heroic measures taken and emergency medicine would not be arriving. Today, his soul would be freed. The space we created would stay sacred. A hearse would be the only additional vehicle in the driveway. Somehow this realization felt reassuring and defined by good planning and kind people. Do Not Resuscitate could sound so harsh and here it felt so grounded for safe passage. Just the night before my husband had helped him down the short hallway from his living room to his bedroom and into his bed for the last time. Forty-five years sleeping in the same room with the same person, and tonight only one would sleep there. Today, he would leave us and his efforts with all the painful options would end. He had refused the wheelchair and the oxygen, and made increasingly limited decisions given the decreasing options and control he continued to hold.

The fluffy flakes kept coming so beautiful and peaceful, like a fairy land for snow-loving unicorns, like a playground for skiers, and nature lovers. Like the beautiful backdrop it was for someone dying. All right outside the window.

My parent's bedroom was small and there weren't enough chairs for the eight of us that were there. We awkwardly moved around the room taking turns being closest as we jockeyed around for space and ideas of what to do. Some moved around the house. A few of us stayed in the room as though we were playing musical chairs. with the resting place being when we sat on the bed next to him, holding his hand and speaking quietly in his ear or listening for his breath which was the only sound he made. His mind seemed lost to the morphine administered by our mom, his constant mate and support. The love of his life.

She was a performer and a teacher. I wondered how giving an injection had gone for her in her newer role. Even as I was in my forties, I saw my mom in a different light, her caretaking and protective nature kicked in, grieving each life change as they moved through each loss little by little, stressors growing bigger. I watched and reflected as she filled her role. Given her productive response to his illness, these last hours could only be imagined. She had fought along with him and had known the battle would end in the loss of her life's love. So sad and unfair.

Seven months prior, they had celebrated their forty-fifth wedding anniversary with live music and friends. They had stolen away to a private hallway away from the group to dance painfully, happily, and lovingly, as they had so many times before this final celebration. Their gratitude showed. The bitterness of that sweet moment still tasted of salty tears. I held the memory in my heart and mind. The love they shared and the loss she suffered was a memory burned in my brain.

Strange coincidences were frequent. Months earlier our dog had been sick. Mega Esophagus was her diagnosis. She would be there with him now. Jim, and Bess the yellow lab. *Would they be in heaven together or over the rainbow bridge? Which one was it?* I wanted to know. Their symptoms paralleled and we were all aware of the strangeness this brought to what was happening to both dad and dog. Bess, my fur baby, had passed first. A strange foreshadowing of what was to come. She was my first baby and fur auntie to our daughters. Our protector. She, the one puking in the driveway, not able to keep food down. She, the one who's ride on this earth had stopped first. Our house was so quiet after she was gone. I brought my mind back into the room.

Inside, I knew that I was there for something sacred, and yet unprepared for, in the Holy Gathering that was playing out in the little bedroom where the core of our family love had lived for so many years. This was our last gathering as we knew it in the sacred space they had created together. A love story of a family of individuals built and living life to its fullest.

My dad was lying awkwardly flat in his bed. *What the hell?* This seemed uncomfortable and weird. *Where was the dying man's pillow? Was dispensing the morphine to him such an awkward task that his pillow was forgotten? Did he not want his pillow?* Do people die without their pillow? Perhaps like sinking down from the morphine he had sunk down into this transition. His chosen hospice nurse had been called and would not arrive for some time yet so we were on our own.

No one had said there would be the giving of any shots or needing the experience of a nurse to tend and care or comfort. These must have been private conversations between my mom and him. I didn't know so I got him a pillow. At least it looked more comfortable for the moment. As if anything would create comfort.

Of the agency he had chosen, he had rejected their hospice support so far. He refused the oxygen and the special equipment. There was one nurse he wanted there for his passing. Her name was Ann. The name of his first grandchild, my daughter. The name of his grandmother he had yet to meet. (He would not know that she had passed on the same date 69 years before.) It would take hospice nurse, Ann, eight hours to get there through the snow. She stopped at her office to pick up supplies and to prepare for this most sacred job. We had counted on her as he had planned. She said she would be there and he would wait.

Gentle snowflakes. Loving beauty as if from heaven. There we were and he had continued to be "surrounded by his loving family." It felt like a role to fill. This unfolded as he had planned while he was in control, organized, and able to follow through with his limited energy. He lived this out and timed his transition with the few options he could hold. We were in our places.

As I sat there and as I watched every breath, I remembered this room as a young child. No one really said much and my mind wandered back to my memories again. I had snuck into the bed, still warm from adult bodies after they rose on weekend mornings before watching cartoons. The bed where I had sucked my thumb secretly/privately, as I soothed/tickled my hand with the satin bindings of different blankets. Satiny ribbon that I had picked away from the woven coarser blankets. Only once had I slept there when my dad had agreed to give up his place for my comfort and reassurance after breaking my arm at age four. Most of life hadn't been a private affair in our family home with five of us there. The one exception was my parent's room. My mom had made that bed every day and liked that no one sat on it. It was their space and a lifetime of respect had been held for that preference. They held an open door policy for most rooms in their house. If the door to their room was closed, it meant that someone was either getting dressed or mad and taking some time. Closed doors were rare and a reason for concern. These and other memories of a lifetime flooded in as I sat in their room that day as I watched the ride that cancer had created, exhale slowly towards a stop. The snow continued as I shot random glances out the window. Although I had lived a life in the snowy climate all of my life, I didn't know that how I saw it would never be the same.

Back into the room, I saw that as he lay there with his forearm propped up at the elbow, his hand made a slow waving motion, back and forth, back and forth. Fingers folded forward as if trying to detect something in the air around him. His eyes were closed and his mostly-quiet body seemed small and frail.

We continued to take turns with him and simply held his hands as his hand continued to move back and forth. His breath slowed and his body seemed to move as though his mind was restless and trying to find peace. *Could it be that by adding predictability to these moments he might calm and be comforted?* I silently considered how this upset in a typical day's routine was impacting his passing. *Was his mind working? If so, how could I help him to calm? What was my role?* No one seemed to know what to do, but to hold his hand and watch.

As a dad and friend, he would want everyone to be "doing their thing." Though in his own pain, I wondered if he might be concerned about us and our children and what we were going through at this time. It would be like him. I wasn't sure but he seemed to relax as I told him what his granddaughters were up to, that the neighbor had walked over to get them. They were at her house with her boys next door eating pancakes with our family's homemade maple syrup. Food from the Wisconsin gods, and from our holy maple trees. Nature's gift of sweet syrup and friends. Routine in the morning ritual of a common day. They were safe. *Was it my imagination or had he calmed slightly?*

More shallow breathing. His son, daughter in law, his best friend and confidant/pastor, his daughter, his other daughter and son in law, his wife—surrounded by his loving family and friends. Had I considered the two pastors' presence more I might reflect on their presence in a more Biblical sense as two high priests in our presence as witnesses. They were authentically human and sad friends just like us. God was definitely in the room and we were connected. The Holy Spirit could be felt closely. We were all there in love. I don't remember last rites, or whatever Lutheran's do, we had all prayed, and the pastor had to leave. The red van backed away from the house reversing by way of the long driveway. The driveway right outside the window. More gentle snow filled the air space.

Now his grandchildren were at the bus stop with more of their neighborhood friends and my dad knew this by my reports. The morning kept on moving for others. Here we stayed. As the pastor drove away, the other women, my mom, my sister, and my sister in law left the room. I was still there as the snow came down in big fluffy flakes. I don't remember what others were saying or doing but again he seemed reassured that his granddaughters had arrived at school. Safe from being home alone, safe with a full belly of pancakes, bacon, and homemade syrup, and safe on the bus ride. His best friend's son was their teacher. The teacher that loved them. The teacher I had known since he was a boy. His dad was my dad's best friend and was in the room with us. His son, the teacher, had been alerted that this was the long anticipated day. He would have physical responsibility for their spiritual well being as come the end of their day, they would receive the sad news. They were in good hands. God was with them and love was in their classrooms. They were safe in their places. So was Jim and so were we. Ann, the hospice nurse. had finally arrived and we had been there for four hours in this one long moment.

My glimpse out the window showed gentle fluffy snowflakes falling to the ground as if they were from the spirits gone before him. They filled the air with flakes of love and peace to calm the earth and to ground for this glorious transition.

As I watched his raised arm wave back and forth like a slow moving flag, I could only imagine the pain and cancer losing out to his outstretched arm which now seemed to be reaching out for heaven, as though he was looking for his loved ones gone as leaders before him. Maybe he had known they were there. It was almost like a radar of some sort searching for the light. Maybe they were reaching in.

As it was me who was closest to him, I leaned in even closer as if to hide the crazy talk and whispered quietly. "It's ok. Bill and Fern, your parents, are there together. They're here for you. You can go now." His hand came down onto his chest, his weakening barely audible breath changed and faded to less audible, almost silent.

Peace was coming. Love was in the room. His body. This life with us. They would be leaving shortly. I felt as though his parents were truly nearby comforting us. Present with the Holy Spirit and urging us all to feel safe in this moment of a life ending for one and profoundly life changing for those left after surrounding him with love on this earth. Along with this feeling and these words of comfort and safety an odor wafted in the room as I first glanced at my dad and then my husband. Unidentifiable, mysterious, and yet familiar to only one other occasion. The birth of our first born. *What is that? Is the smell of death actually the scent of birth?* Questions and connections filled my brain and nose as this scent lingered as familiar. A clean fresh scent, another strange sign.

His body was letting go. It felt damp and I knew he would want fresh boxers. As I looked around the room, I realized I was the only woman left. I would try not to make this awkward. But it was. The guys and me. Hopefully I was leading the right action. As we gingerly worked together to move his fragile body we agreed to change his pants. As we gently peeled away his comfy pajamas, his wrinkled penis came into view. This was unexpected. Oh my. I had to hold off my laughter. *What was I helping with? Why had I stayed? What the hell?!* This wasn't what I wanted to remember from this solemn time. So memorably normal as the once little girl who had busted into a bathroom. As the little girl who had gotten showers from her dad, the health teacher, the person that had taught her all of the biologically correct labels of body parts, male and female. Who had taught her safety, respect, and dignity, and boundaries. Memories of a summer day when he had taken my jr. high friend and I out for an afternoon of sailing on his small sailboat. The time when my friend and I had awkwardly stared at each other, as the elephant in the sailboat had been his penis staring at us as it drooped out of his infamous gym shorts. After many tacks across the lake, he had finally looked down and noticed. Looking up at us pubescent girls he had calmly and awkwardly said, "Has that been like that for a long time?" Here it was again. Not at all how I'd imagined death would look.

The hospice nurse helped us and brought things back to changing his clothes. He was closer to the next phase where clothes wouldn't be needed, where he wouldn't know and he wouldn't care just as he had said. "I won't know or care. I'll be dead."

He was gone. Ann checked for a heartbeat. There we sat. Trying to hold on.

Coincidently or not, another sign that God was working magic and mystery, my friend was checking in on the phone and the medical equipment delivery guy was at the door to drop off oxygen and a wheelchair. They would not be needed. He felt bad as my dad had just passed and his timing might have seemed to interrupt. The perfection of the moment he had unknowingly created wasn't lost. He and the medical equipment were gone as quickly as they had arrived. The cancer was gone and so was my dad.

> The perfection of the moment he had unknowingly created wasn't lost.

His soul and his body were free from the disease and its needs. The linens were changed and there was a freshness in the air. We tenderly prepared him to leave. The funeral director arrived and we directed him to fresh boxers, a clean t-shirt, my dad's best suit, a shave, and a trim of any random hairs left on his head. God was with us and so was the spirit of our loved ones gone too soon. They were most likely present in the expensive and short three-quarter mile ride to the funeral home. The car seemed to be full of love and abundance. I could still feel the presence of his parents' spirit in the cloud of love around us as we stood and watched the hearse drive away.

He was free to float with his ancestors and the angels. I had helped them connect. They showed themselves to me daily as the fluffy snowflakes fell, as the wind blew through the leaves in the trees, and as the birds flew by.

Later that week, on our daughter's birthday and the anniversary of my grandma's passing, as I walked into the funeral home I was taken by all of the beautiful flower arrangements from so many friends and pockets of my dad's existence. As I came to the last arrangement, a white poinsettia from two generations of close family friends, I was drawn to the card whose signature included "Fern and Bill."

The next day we stood in the front row of the church, the eight of us, separate and not alone, from the rest of the full church of about five-hundred. My dad was a good man. I had been blessed. We sang out loud and strong to celebrate his life well lived while we strengthened ourselves and many others.

Weeks later, the grief loaded in like a pile of unshoveled snow, heavy cold and wet. I appreciated the devastated feeling as I found my way to the basement to grieve privately and away from the family hovering in the living room above me. *The lower the low, the higher the high*, I thought. Although sometimes loud in my ways of expression, I wanted to muffle the sounds of my cries.

I found a basket of laundry on the floor next to the washing machine, stuck my head in, and wailed. The high had come earlier that day while sitting in my new finished upper attic master bedroom, my dad's dream and our recent reality. He had been able to sit with me there just once. With a clear blue sky outside and while sitting in my beautiful new chair talking to my college roommate, I had cried soft and gentle tears reminiscing about our dads and our conversations back as nineteen-year-olds wondering how we would live without them someday. As we spoke, fluffy glistening bright white snowflakes floated by my window through the shining afternoon sun. The sky was so clear. *What the hell was going on?* A beautiful, sunshiny, clear-blue day, and that ever mysterious snow randomly visible. The unpredictable reminder that our dads were with us in spirit some thirty years later.

Joy Danner Lehman

Joy Danner Lehman is committed to learning how to simply "be" after a full career as a speech/language pathologist in the public schools where she learned to communicate with the souls of her students and their families whose rich diversity brought color and culture to the tapestry of her life. She continues to emerge into her next life as a lightworker and an author after years of feeling called to serve and empower others.

She's parented two daughters as a working mom and recently celebrated thirty years of marriage to the same person! She wants to grow into the role of a transformational life coach and retreat leader as she processes through the growing pains of reflecting on life experiences of light and those from the shadows as well.

Joy received her Master in Science Degree, she held a Certificate of Clinical Competence with the American Speech Language and Hearing Association for over 30 years, and was a certified ski instructor. She also works as an independent consultant for Rodan and Fields because she loves taking great care of herself at home and sharing those benefits with her friends.

CONNECT WITH JOY

 @4joy153 	joy4yourskin.myrandf.com

CHAPTER 12

She's An Eagle When She Flies

By Whisper James

I was sprawled, staring at the roof, trying to focus on dots of…*something?* I couldn't tell what they were because my eyes wouldn't focus and when they did, the dots multiplied.

My body was airbourne for less than a tenth of a second, but it still came down hard. *Where are we? Is this a dirt road?*

A sudden turn. This time, my body slid on the slick, white leather seat. I knew it was leather because the Man driving had made sure to tell us it was. At least twice. I was not impressed at all. It still felt like plastic, and I was sliding on it just like plastic.

My mind stumbled into why fur turned to plastic once it's off the animal. It was not a coherent thought. Perhaps it was all the glasses of bubbly wine the driver had insisted I drink that were now sloshing around my brain. Or perhaps it was because I was only ten.

(You didn't read that wrong. I was ten, and drunk.)

My head was still sloshing, but I could hear the Auntie in the passenger seat, "You know, you shouldn't have given her all that wine. Her mother may get upset at you."

He snorted. "Do you think that I care?" I knew what he meant. He wasn't one of my mom's "Fish." Of course, he could be if he wanted to. He was one of the "Big Fish." The special ones who were rich or powerful enough. This one was rich. A Big Fish could visit any of the Homes at any time and have his choice of...companions.

That's how I ended up here, in the back of a Mercedes, sprawled on white leather seats, trying to remember if I was remembering.

The car took a sharp left. I was not about to slide onto that fucking floor again. Instinctively, I grabbed hold of the seat cushion. My fingers touched something plastic. I pulled it out. It was a white cassette tape.

My eyes widened. "Dolly Parton's Greatest Hits," I read silently. I had never heard of her, but that, of course, was because I'd never heard of anyone. (Except Michael Jackson. I did know who that was, but only because in the early 80s he was EVERYWHERE. Even in Malaysia, where I was drunk and bounce-sliding around in the backseat of a car like I was in a snow globe.)

Holding the cassette tape, I was suddenly sober. Or, it felt like that because the blood had drained from my brain to help my heart beat. I was holding something from the *Outside World*.

* * *

There was a reason I'd never heard of anyone, anywhere.

I was born into and raised in the notorious cult, the Children of God. Their later aliases have been The Family of Love, The Family, and The Family International, respectively. (Yeah, some geniuses at work there.)

The Children of God is a "fundamental" Christian, apocalyptic, isolationist cult. It's better known in the news as a sex cult, and they definitely use "fundamental" incorrectly.

If your curiosity is anything like mine, you'll probably want to toss those names into a search engine (Protip: "Children of God" works best). But be ready. There's a lot of information out there about them. Unfortunately, nothing good. (Unless you end up on their website. That information is—miraculously—super good.)

The Children of God came to be in 1968, when a handful of disenchanted, hippie teens followed a fifty-year-old disgraced Evangelical preacher and his children into a clubhouse and declared a "revolution against the System."

In the post-Vietnam War era, they found plenty of disenchanted hippie teens. By the early 70s, they had grown to a point of requiring their members to report their numbers. By 1973, they had four thousand Members, five hundred eighty Homes[1], were in sixty-two Countries, and one hundred twenty-two babies had been born.

That's when I came on to the scene. I was one of the one hundred twenty-two.

Growing up in the Children of God, we were raised in institutionalized abuse. As in, all the physical, sexual, emotional, mental, and spiritual abuses you could think of… but make them institutionalized. No matter what Home you went to, you would experience the same abuses. Nothing changed, just the faces.

Isolation from the outside world—the "System"—was one of the strictest held rules. Going out into the System required intense and unrelenting supervision of at least two adults. No System school, music, books, movies, friends, jobs, relatives. No contact at all. None. No

---

[1] Homes: the cult's name for communes

exceptions, unless you were proselytizing or asking for money. So, if you did speak to a Systemite[2], *it better be about Jesus!*

That's why it was such a big deal when I decided to risk everything to sneak the cassette tape home.

● ● ●

I spent the rest of the ride trying to look like I was sleeping, while imagining my once-in-a-lifetime private Dolly Parton show, and begging Jesus for forgiveness.

Just for one listen, Jesus, I promise to put it back.

I knew I could promise that, because I knew I'd be in this backseat again.

Or bed. Or hotel room.

Luckily, it wasn't going to happen to me that night. When we got to the Man's house, the Auntie[3] said I was too drunk for anything and sent me to the living room—or some room with a couch.

I tumbled onto his couch. *Oh, for fucks sake. What was it with this guy and leather seating? So, no bedding?* The Auntie wasn't the nurturing type. She didn't have to be, she was a star FFer[4], and one of the few allowed to be childless.

She leaned in so close, I could smell her fish dinner mixed with alcohol. *Gross.* Exhausted, I curled deeper into my knees and pretended to sleep. "Whisper?" I squeezed my eyes tighter until I heard her suck her teeth. She was preparing to hiss through them. "You better not have done anything to make the Man angry."

---

[2] Systemite: Someone who lived in the System (outside world).
[3] Any woman who was a member of the cult.
[4] FF: short for "Flirty Fishing;" aka proselytizing and getting money for the cult through prostitution. Fish were the men they targeted

The fish-whiskey smell left with the Auntie, and I started breathing for what felt like the first time that night. My cheek against the cold, plastic-leather, I didn't care that there was no pillow or blanket. With chattering teeth, I clutched my cassette tape tightly. In that moment, nothing else mattered. Not tonight. **There would be other nights and other "Mans." But not tonight.** The bubbles in my head were quieter now. Or they had all popped. *Not tonight.*

In the morning, the couch was still plasticky and cold. Those bubbles had definitely all popped. *Why is my entire body a nauseated stomach? Never mind.* I dared for a moment to touch my tape. It was still there, wrapped in my sweater like a roti. *Bleh. No rotis.* But I smiled through the queasiness; I had Dolly. I couldn't have known what that tape was going to mean to me. Or maybe I did, the way it already felt like a treasure. I was giddy all the way home. Going back to where every tomorrow was worse than every today, I knew I could bear it better now.

I had Dolly.

●　●　●

I always smile when I recall my triumphant ride home. I never did put that cassette tape back.

Getting away with smuggling the contraband tape into my life would end up being my salvation many times over. It was something that was mine, and only mine. In that chaotic, confused world I was growing up in, it felt like a lifeline to sanity.

Dolly stayed with me over the years, while that Man faded into the darkness, just like the many other men before him and the many men that would come after him.

Okay

If you feel like you need a few deep breaths, that's okay. I have to take a breather sometimes too. (And it's *my* story. But, yes it's a lot.)

It's also okay if this is freaking you the fuck out. This isn't supposed to be okay. None of this was okay. A 10-year-old isn't supposed to know what being drunk tastes like. She shouldn't have understood that she was meant to ask for gold jewelry when she went with the Man(s) and that she was the trade for the gold.

If that leaves your brain screaming, and your heart begging to look away, it's a good thing. It means you are sane. The people who I grew up around were not.

I still get surprised at the levels of depraved insanity that was everyday life for me. With casual resignation I'd accepted I'd be given out to the Man again, but it was my "sin" of wanting to listen to the tape that had me trembling, bargaining with chips a little girl should never have to hold.

I didn't know then that my eventual attempts to fuse this cult god I knew with a supposed god of love would prove spiritually fatal. I think I gave up trying to understand the cult's god and why he would be so angry at the gentle wishes of a little girl, but that she would please him as crippled prey. What I did know was that the worn journey from my knees for their prayers to my knees for their phallic pacifiers was a short one.

Would it help if I took a moment to skip to the good part? It's this: *I'm okay.* I'm on the other side of these particular storms. The woman I am today is a Warrior who is proud of her scars.

I wouldn't write about my story if I wasn't. But it's not easy to read, I know. It's not easy to write. I guess that's partly why I throw some humor in.

So if anything makes you chuckle, that's okay. If you find nothing funny at all, that's also okay. (Just don't write to me about it.)

This is not to minimize anything. It was shockingly ugly what happened to so many of us. But sometimes I need to laugh. It makes my monsters a little smaller and their shadows fall a little shorter.

She Must Have Written It For Me

One of the songs on Dolly's tape was "*The Bargain Store.*" These days it's probably not one of Dolly's more recognized songs, but it was one of the ones I played over, and over and over again. From the first night I brought her home, under my headphones, I would listen to Dolly's lilting, glittery voice singing my song to me, and I would thank her with snot and tears.

The words that were "mine" said:

My life is like a bargain store
I may have just what you're looking for
If you don't mind the fact that all the merchandise is used
With a little mending it could be as good as new.

I say "mine" because there were times where I felt so broken, I would pretend that she had written it about me. With my thumbnail years and my poor orphaned heart, I would wonder if someone could ever come along to love me, now that I was so used up. Used up, in my all-of-ten-years-old. It wouldn't be until years later that I would understand that a ten, eleven, or twelve year old wasn't meant to think they were "used up."

That little girl is the reason I have held on through hurricanes, undone monsters, and plowed through hell to ensure my children will never know this cycle. From these wounds I sourced a typhoon of unconditional acceptance, and a love without edges that will always be theirs. I transformed my abandoned little girl into their unwavering Warrior.

That little girl is the reason I have held on through hurricanes, undone monsters, and plowed through hell

As sad as it was that I had seen so much pain and abuse that I could believe those lyrics were for me, still, my soul was telling me that this wasn't love. It was registering as very wrong, even though I'd never known anything else. I like to thank Dolly for this, but obviously something in me knew. My heart was rejecting the abuse, even when my conscious mind couldn't picture living another way.

The Necklace

There finally came the time that we would leave that country behind. The country that brought me so much pain, so much confusion, and to so many men, would be gone.

I remember it so clearly.

• • •

They said the leadership wanted us to move to a new country. My heart nearly jumped out of my chest. I didn't care about the reason. We'd moved so many times already, my passport looked like a United Nations conference. I only cared about one thing. *I wouldn't have to see the Worst Man again.*

No, not the Always-Leather-Seats Man who would get me drunk. This Man was so much worse than all the other dripping, wrinkled men. My body convulsed at the thought.

So, how soon can we leave?

I didn't need to ask that. I could blink, and our world would be packed up yet again. We had practice. Lots. (Is there such a thing as a professional packer? Ask me to pack a suitcase. I will tetris the shit out of that and fill it with twice as much as you can.)

Am I watching one of those Charlie Chaplin movies? You know the ones, where everything is going just a little too fast, but not so fast that it's on fast forward. I wanted to be on fast forward. I knew that I wanted to get out of this country—so very, very badly—but what was the rush for everyone else? *Maybe they are afraid of something too.*

I was counting down the seconds until I'd be gone from the blackest place I had ever lived. Unfortunately, I wasn't the only one counting down.

The Worst Man was too. Another Big Fish, only he was the scariest of all. I had been traded to him the most. The most gold jewelry was from him, and the most pain. I thought of how often he would tell me that I belonged to him. Sometimes I believed him, since nothing seemed to stop him.

But leaving would...right? I felt relief watching his eyes flash when he found out I would soon be out of reach. I was so glad. In my mind I was soaring where I would be safe from him. *Yes, I know there will be more Uncles[5], but at least not him.*

---

[5] Uncles: Any man who was a member of the cult.

Except he was showing up more than usual. *Maybe because we're leaving?* I am terrified he is going to ask for one last trade. I want to not be here. *Can I pray for that?* My heart was exhausted. I curled up into my bed. I needed to cry, to hear her voice. I put my headphones on, and pressed play on my Walkman. I would imagine that I was Sandy, and Dolly would take me in for my last night. I wanted to not be here anymore. *Ain't ya got an extra bed for me and little Andy?*

She was just a little girl, not more than six or seven
But that night as they slept the angels took them both to heaven
God knew little Andy would be lonesome with her gone
Now Sandy and her puppy dog won't ever be alone

We were leaving, in days, then in hours.

The Worst Man showed up on the last day. This time he didn't care who saw the way he grabbed my arms, and I froze from the shock of that. His hands were so tight, I was sure he had reached my bones. Suddenly he pushed something into my hand.

"You are mine, and you always will be. Wear this so you know you belong to me. I will follow and find you."

All the soaring miles in my head suddenly turned to inches. My feet were sinking in mud. It was not a small or vain threat. The Worst Man was a very top-ranking member of the military, the same military that ran the country.

I looked at my hand, even though I already knew. A gold necklace. But it was different this time. My blood suddenly felt cold inside me. The Worst Man had carved his name on it.

●　●　●

For the first few years after we arrived in Thailand, on the rare occasion I would be outside one of the Homes, I would scan every face looking for the Worst Man. I would see him on sidewalks and around corners. None of my body parts ever stayed where they were supposed to. I would hear my stomach in my ears and feel my heart pumping in my throat.

It was exhausting always being so terrified. One day I was so tired, I simply decided that the Worse Man was dead. I imagined his fat stomach drowning his heart and that in the last moment he'd know I had finally hated him hard enough. I stopped being afraid of him. I hoped the maggots took their time with his rot, but he would never touch *me* again. (I still won't watch James Bond movies, or listen to Nat King Cole, but I call that a win/win.)

Like an invisible collar, that necklace stayed with me, years after it had been taken and sold. My own markless branding.

During those pre-teen years, the Worst Man was my scariest nightmare, the one who could leave me trembling in fear, so much more than my dad or the Uncles would. Perhaps because he was part of the *Outside World*, the System. What I've found over the years is that the wounds from the Worst Man have long since faded, while it was the ones who were supposed to love me, whose betrayal left the truly lasting scars and the deepest branding.

To Thailand and the Wheel of Terror

I turned twelve a few weeks after arriving in Thailand. An adult, according to the cult. That meant full responsibility. It meant I could drink wine. I'm sure there were more "allowances," but the one that mattered to me was that I was allowed to watch the few adult cult-approved movies. Like Star Trek.

My happiness at turning twelve was short-lived. A handful of movies were a pitiful compensation for the shitshow those next few years turned out to be. Becoming an "adult" at twelve sounded good to us, but apparently there was the fine print. Really, really shitty fine print.

I don't think there's a better way to describe it: I was a ward of the cult. Passed around as they saw fit, from one Home to another, whenever it would suit a purpose. What purpose? Whose purpose? I never knew. Truthfully, a reasoning wouldn't have made a difference. "I gave you to God," my mom responded when I had written to her and asked why they had sent me away. In two years, I was moved to, and from, six different Homes. Weirdly, it was both confusing and comforting that a move would only change the faces. Of course, there was always some fresh hell unique to that Home—but the essence remained the same.

Even today, many of my nightmares are filled with dozens of people I'm aware I am living with, and I never know any of them. A Home was required to have anywhere from twenty-five to forty-five people, and I wasn't the only one being moved around all the time. Especially the young teens like me; they never seemed to really know what to do with us.

Except make us work. When we weren't being indoctrinated, we were a full-time workforce. From childcare, to fundraising, to cooking—all of it—,we were free labor they could crush into submission. "Trafficking" was definitely not a word they would have used. (They will still vehemently claim that wasn't what it was.)

Naively, when I left Malaysia, I thought I'd left behind the worst of my sexual abuse. *I passed the threshold*, I thought. Instead, there was the shitty fine print. I don't think I could forget the day I first found out the *full* requirements of being a twelve-year-old adult.

• ● ●

A sledgehammer could have dropped on my toe as I stood there and I wouldn't have felt it. I was staring at the Wheel of Terror. I was on it. I had only moved here four days ago, and I was staring at my name. On the Wheel. I was on the Wheel. I guess I need to get used to this, real fast.

This is really not worth a Star Trek movie and a glass of wine, was all I could think.

• ● ●

The (actual) adults called it the Sharing[6] Schedule. To me, and the other few pre-teens around, it was the Wheel of Terror. I loathed it. I never could adapt to it or endure it. I wish I had known that it never should have been something I was required to "adapt" to.

Usually within days of getting to a new Home, my name would be added to the Wheel. The men were on the outside wheel, the females on the inside (there were *always* more men than women), and it would hang on the Home's main bulletin board. Every week it would be turned, and that would be your Sharing partner for that week. You know, sharing god's love. Penises as the conduit, of course.

The School That Actually Wasn't

I was fifteen when the cult decided to open "schools" to house and control (er, "train") the insane amounts of kids they were having. Take a movement that promoted boundary-free sex with as many possible women the men

---

[6] Sharing was initially used to describe swinging (as in "sharing your partner") and evolved into a generic term for sex.

could find, combine that with never allowing birth control or protection, and herpes wasn't the only thing running rampant. Eight thousand eight hundred thirteen of us had been born into exploitation by the year I turned fifteen.

(Oh, and the herpes thing? Not hyperbole. It was not uncommon for the Homes to have a "herpes bathroom" for outbreak season.)

They heralded it as the "School Vision." (Although "Boarding School Vision" would have been more accurate.) The one in Thailand was called the Training Center, or "TC" for short, and the property we were housed in was an old, broken-down hospital. There were always somewhere between two hundred to two hundred fifty-250 people living there, and it wasn't uncommon to pass someone in the hall you hadn't seen for six days, because you were on kitchen duty and they were cleaning toilets.

The years I spent there were painful ones. They may have turned the sex abuse volume down (well, *told* people they turned it down), but they turned all the physical, mental, psychological, and spiritual abuse volume way, way up. Like a neighbour kid who stopped playing the drums at 2 a.m., only to add an entire band and amplifier.

There's no need to tell all the stories of mindfuckery and abuse that happened at the School That Wasn't A School. In today's spotlight, some of our experiences would be similar to stories from the infamous "Troubled Teen Industry," but even that feels dismissive and inaccurate.

We were prisoners in their war against their own children.

Over those dark years, I would listen to Dolly (when I could get away with it), her angelic voice carrying me to places I'd never known. When the insanity seemed sure to drown me, she was a tether to sanity. Her voice sang to me of places in this world, somewhere, where children were safe and loved and cared for.

I'm going to fast forward a bunch as I attempt to condense several years into a few lines, but by the end of my time at the School That Wasn't A School, I was a young kid, pregnant without choices or options, engaged to an even-younger kid who, at seventeen, was going to become a father.

The Everywhere and Nowhere

We were sent to a Home in upcountry Thailand. It was probably the most rural town I'd lived in. (Not been in, just lived in.) There were several adults, handfuls of kids; mostly strangers. Almost immediately, I became very sick. "Morning sickness," they rolled their eyes. No. No, something was wrong. In a cult adamantly opposed to secular medicine and doctors, trying to get any help other than prayer was screaming at the ocean.

I got sicker. What I didn't know at the time was that I have Hyperemesis gravidarum (HG), an extreme type of morning sickness that can be fatal to both mom and baby. In fact, until the 1950s, it was the leading cause of maternal death.

It nearly became mine.

● ● ●

Okay, where am I? I was so confused. *Am I being punished?* I was in a wheelchair. *Oh, I remember now!* I couldn't stand up any longer; my legs were crumpling under me each time I tried. No one from the Home was anywhere to be seen. We had committed the unforgivable by going to a hospital, so they had just dumped us off at the front doors. They didn't even leave a note in my basket. I clung to the plastic pitcher I'd carried with me everywhere for the last three months. Except it wasn't just bile I was throwing up anymore, it was blood.

I still didn't know what was happening, mainly because no one in the hospital spoke English. Except for one doctor, and he was two days away. They wheeled me to a room with eleven women, all moms in some stage of pre- or post-delivery. The whole hospital was the same colour, I thought. There were too many voices garbling in my head. There was a drain in the middle of the room. *Yikes.* I had been to places like this, to sing at for our one missionary act of the month. *Now I'm a patient here.*

My poor baby husband, barely eighteen, was trembling like a chihuahua as I was weaving in and out of consciousness. I cried for him...or I was crying because I needed to pee. I remember wanting to pee. My body refused to cooperate with the condensed metal toilet, so I decided to get out of bed. To walk to the bathroom, of course, as if my body was working at all. Many things happened, most of them all at once. So many voices...and then,

Silence.

I am nowhere. But, also, everywhere. I registered that I didn't seem to have form. In a rush, like a bullet train, I felt it come in, flooding me: total, complete peace. There isn't a word for...all this. *I feel full, happy, expanding, infinite. I have never felt anything close to this, and I never want to let it go. I can feel everyone. All of me and them and love. So much love. Unending love.*

So this is what dying feels like; a soft sigh. Okay, I'm ready.

I understood that all I would have to do is let go and I would become one with this. My part of it becoming a whole of it. I felt what I imagined a balloon just let go of would feel, in that moment before it flies.

Then there was a flicker of him. *Hmm, him.* In the expansion was a center that reverberated. Pulsed. *My baby.* I felt his want, more than his need. *No, need is there, but I feel the want. He wants me to stay for him.*

Okay, little one, me too. You deserve that chance.

I felt breath. Everything that was nothing became nothing. I heard Thai voices again. and...*FUCKING HELL! The pain! Is this really how much pain lives here? I am SO heavy, an elephant is sitting on me. Hurting. Every inch of me, every bone.*

It looked like it was day. I thought it was night. I look at my watch. *WHAT HAPPENED TO MY WATCH?!* I couldn't even see the hands, the glass was so shattered. Then I saw the bruises. Everywhere, covering my arms, my legs. Somebody had invited me to Fight Club but didn't tell me. My infant husband had a look on his face. "What happened?" I asked. At least, I think I did.

"You kind of... left us," he said. My head didn't feel all the way there. Like it was a pie missing 3 pieces. *Come again?*

Oh. OH! I put my hand over my abdomen. *Yes, baby, I'm going to give you every possible chance.*

* * *

So much changed after my time in the Everywhere and Nowhere. I knew, without a doubt, that I needed to rescue my baby from this life. I hadn't even taken in the enormity of what had happened yet.

A couple of weeks later, I received a letter from the one precious thing I found in the cult: my BFF. (Ah, the days of snail mail.) It was dated the morning after the Everywhere and Nowhere happened. Her letter said I had come to her during the night and told her she was going to get some news that I was sick, but everything was going to be okay.

Sometimes it feels like I *still* have goosebumps from that letter. The enormity finally caught up: I was never going back.

Breaking Free

In 1996, I flew to the U.S. It was clear I wasn't going to be able to keep my baby healthy or safe unless I did. We were swallowed up into yet another Home almost immediately (what would be the first of several) and what followed were five long years of pain, confusion, and depression.

For me, that is. My infant husband, why, he was having a grand time, including carrying on a three-year-long relationship with a woman and also having sex with the other women in the Home. I gave up being hurt by it after the Third Exorcism they'd given me for being hurt by it. He was—to no one's surprise—very comfortable in the cult. But I was living a nightmare. I had four kids who somehow seemed to be all the same age. I'd had a miscarriage alone in my bathtub. I wasn't allowed to learn to drive or have money, making me dependent on the infant husband, even with his three-year relationship.

I thought I was terrified of becoming a single mom with a deck so stacked against me. But truthfully, I had forgotten my strength.

After those five years, I finally convinced the kids' father to escape with the kids and me. We weren't allowed to have any money ourselves unless we were going to the "mission field," so we told the leadership we were. Once we got the money, we secretly bought round trip tickets from New York to Kingston, Jamaica.

We were flying out of JFK on September 11th, 2001. Except for an embarrassed travel agent messing up one of our tickets, we would have been sitting in JFK when the towers fell. We left from LaGuardia on Sept 15th instead.

After five months in Jamaica, the futile attempt to establish an orphanage collapsed under government regulations. We flew back to NY on February 18, 2002, with only $500 to our name. We were offered a room in the basement of an upstate NY house, assuming we could get there.

After a $300 taxi ride, in a tiny basement room with $200, and four kids under six, my life started for the first time.

Me, I'll Just Be Fine

Lord, it's like a hard candy Christmas
I'm barely getting through tomorrow,
But still I won't let sorrow bring me way down.

My life since leaving the cult has been much more like the scrambled strings of Christmas lights than the cliche "ups and downs." And like those tangled strings of lights, there have been many starts and stops, blown fuses, and mostly not knowing which end was up.

Getting out of the destructive cult I had been born into has been overwhelming and confusing and challenging and inspiring. All the things. These days, this is the part of my life I usually want to talk about. It's the part that was the toughest and the most rewarding; the part that matters the most to me. It's where I ended the cycle of abuse and brought my kids into a world of unconditional love and freedom.

In the podcast I started and host with my BFF, I talk a lot about my life since leaving. It's even in the title: *Butterflies and Bravery: Leaving, Living and Loving After A Cult.* The fulfillment, expansion, and love that I've experienced since starting my podcast has been immeasurable. In telling my story, I've turned my past into purpose.

As you can imagine, there is a lot of story not captured in this condensed chapter, and some not even touched on. I've got stories of starting over, kids, divorce, suicides, deaths, coming out, discovery, and a life of healing. In the end, finding the cassette tape of Dolly's songs was the place that I wanted to jump off from. I even thought I knew why.

As one of my most vivid memories, it's a place I return to when I think about influences in my life, and what I often think of as the beginning. The beginning because it was the first time I fully understood there was something beyond the cornered walls the cult had boxed around me.

It was my first connection to hope.

Although I didn't know it at the time, carrying that tape of Dolly's songs through so many years of pain and abuse kept a connection to the center of my soul, the part that believed in a better world. But in writing this chapter, I realized I had touched something even deeper.

It was my power. In having the bravery to risk so much for something for myself, I tapped into my power for the first time. Believing in something more, I acted on it. It wasn't just Dolly (who I love) that I had taken home that night, but also a reminder that I had believed in something better for me, and it had made me brave.

Even if just for a moment, I had imagined a better world where children are loved, valued and safe, and I responded with courage. That's why it's my beginning; it was the first time I felt my power.

So, what gave me that bravery? It was more than just believing that gave me the courage to step into that power. It was because I had acknowledged my worth. I had believed in the possibility of a better life, and not just that it was possible, but that it was possible for *me*. I deserved love and safety, and that gave me the courage to be brave.

Belief, Then Worth, Then Power

That's when I saw the connection.

Belief, worth, and power are all connected, and one feeds the other—they all need each other. Just believing in something is not enough, but if you believe in that something for you, *That's your worth agreeing with you.*

I'll use the example of wanting a better job. You have to first *believe* that the job is out there, then you have to believe that it's for you, that you are *worthy* of the job, and that in turn gives you the courage to take your *power* and go get the job.

In some ways it's very simple, each step creating the building block for the next one. But also, sometimes it's not so simple, because you still have to take that next step. It might start with a question, or a hope. A question or hope is neutral. But if from that question or hope you can envision something more for you, take it and use it to see your worthiness. If you want something, doesn't that say that your soul knows you are worthy of having it? Belief is the steppingstone that you can use to show yourself your own worth. Then from your worth, step into your power, and make it happen.

That's why I kept coming back to the story of finding Dolly's tape. The moment I first believed that there was something better that I deserved, it helped me feel brave enough to bring the tape home.

I am often asked, "How are you still here, how did you survive through everything?" I don't know if there's really one answer for that. But maybe part of it was that, in the backseat of a white Mercedes, at ten years old, I met my power for the first time, and I took that Warrior home with me.

Shaped like a white Dolly Parton cassette tape, I've carried my moment of courage and power with me all along.

But Am I Worth It?

Living with trauma and C-PTSD often means living with a lot of challenges. (It sure does for me.) You're on a path of healing, and you may also have mental health issues or addiction, there are triggers and coping and masking, and making sure, in all that, that you are productive, present, and show up for life.

It's a lot.

But how do you know you're *worthy*? Through all the work and counseling and healing I've done, for me, that is the hardest one—that's the doozy. Living with trauma can completely cripple any feelings of worth. So, how do you go about finding it? You can't just pull it out of the air. (Tried that.) You can't just pull it out of your ass. (I am trusting that doesn't work either.) In reality, most humans need validation to believe in our own worth, and how do we validate ourselves?

I saw the steps: belief, then worth, then power. In recognizing the building blocks of these steps from belief to power, I realized that this could be the key to finding that worth. Once I believe it, then I can also believe that I deserve it. *That I'm worthy.*

When you believe something is possible, if you can picture it and desire it, you already know you're worthy. And once you connect to your worth, that's when your Warrior kicks in and says, *Let's go get it.*

Believing something is possible for you is your soul knowing you're worthy of it.

This is why I go back to the tape. My soul, she knows. She knows that was the start of my story of reclamation and power. And she gave me the building blocks for knowing my worth.

My belief became my worth became my power.

She's been there, God knows she's been there

She has seen and done it all

She's a woman, she knows how to dish it out or take it all

Her heart's as soft as feathers, still she weathers stormy skies

And she's a sparrow when she's broken

But she's an eagle when she flies

Gentle as the sweet magnolia, strong as steel her faith and pride

She's an everlasting shoulder, she's a leading post of life

She hurts deep, and when she weeps, she's just as fragile as a child

And she's a sparrow when she's broken

But she's an eagle when she flies

– DOLLY PARTON

Whisper James

Hi, I'm Whisper James.

I grew up in a rather unconventional way, by which I mean that my passport is American, my parents are from Ireland, and I had lived in fourteen countries and countless cities before I was twenty.

All the circus living I've done so far has left me quite good at juggling, which I am doing quite a bit of lately. I am Director of Community Engagement for i-5 Freedom Network, a non-profit organization fighting Human Trafficking. I also work part-time in the publishing world with self-publishing authors, and do occasional graphic and web design. Best of all, I am the founder and co-host of a weekly podcast of Survivor voices called Butterflies and Bravery.

I've been lucky enough to be called mom by four amazing kids, who've now grown and flown. Besides my four kids, I have eighteen siblings, (sixteen of them are half-siblings), one dog, and a part-time cat. (She travels a lot.) The beach is what makes my heart smile, and I am an artist in my spare time (Which is obviously not much.) I am curious as to where more writing might take me.

It's incredible to have a future to look forward to.

CONNECT WITH WHISPER

 @whisperwjames  butterfliesandbravery.com

Conclusion

By Jolie Dawn

To witness another woman share the depths of her pain, and to be witnessed in her vulnerability, is nothing short of a miracle. For many generations of women on the planet, sharing in this way was not only not possible, it simply wasn't safe. It is a true blessing to be alive in a time in history where women get the opportunity to support each other as we do now.

It says a lot about the type of woman that you are to be receiving the wisdom of this book. A fellow brave woman, rule-breaker, change-maker, devotee to a life of light and growth. With deep respect, I bless your journey of life ahead.

May these words ring in your head with messages of hope, inspiration, and encouragement when you need them most. May you return to this book in the moments where life feels like it twisted you sideways and you seek to remember that standing firmly on both feet is just one breath away. May you remember this truth "if she can do it, I can do it."

Each author in this book has opened an invitation for you to connect with her personally, if you feel called. At the end of each chapter is the author's bio and links to connect further. If you were touched by a particular story, I invite you to make contact with the author. She would love to hear from you.

To each author in this book, Alison Tugwell, Chotsani Sackey, Laura Lee Lotto, Simerjit (Sim) Sethi, Mary Lancaster, Joy Danner Lehman, Jen Miller, Ivy Kaminsky, Jennifer Wreyford, Christy (Chi Chi) Yip, Wiaam Yasin, Whisper James, Amanda Goolsby: I thank you from the bottom of my heart. Your bravery and courage will inspire me for the rest of my time on the planet and beyond. I know first-hand how edgy it feels to have your story be witnessed.

If sharing your story and becoming a published author is calling to you, please head to joliedawn.com and look for Creatrix Publishing. We are accepting submissions for co-authors in our upcoming volumes of Dare to Express. It would be a joy to support the sharing of *your* story.

*Dare to be the greatness that
you came to Earth to be.*

Dare to be the Creatrix of your own story.

*Dare to share the wisdom of
your life experience.*

Dare to be seen in your raw truth.

Dare to Express.

Made in the USA
Las Vegas, NV
16 September 2022

Thank you for reading this book.

It is our hope that what you read here touched and inspired you.
If you resonated with one or more of the stories within these pages,
please leave a review on Amazon.